Cybersecurity
for Everyone

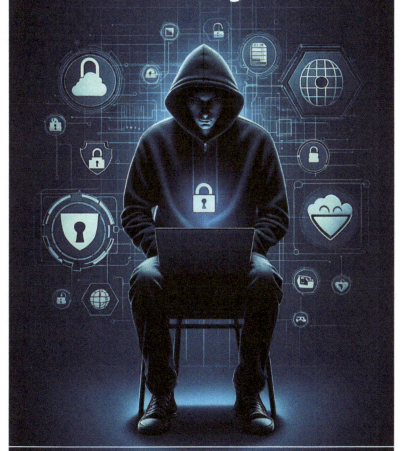

Unlocking Cybersecurity: From Beginner to Expert

Marc

ABOUT THE AUTHOR

Mr.Marc (Dhanasekaran) is a distinguished IT professional with over 18 years of experience in digital transformation and AI integration. He is a Senior Director of Engineering, leading significant projects that enhance operational excellence and technological innovation. His work primarily focuses on migrating legacy systems to modern cloud architectures and implementing effective risk management strategies.

An author and educator in artificial intelligence, Mr.Marc has written "Artificial Intelligence for Everyone" to make AI technologies accessible to a wide audience. His book aims to simplify complex AI concepts and demonstrate their practical applications in everyday life. With a Bachelor of Engineering in Electrical & Electronics and an Oracle Certified Professional Java Programmer certification, his career showcases rapid progression and substantial achievements in technology leadership.

Follow on Linkedin:- https://www.linkedin.com/in/dhana10/

INTRODUCTION: WHY CYBERSECURITY MATTERS

In the digital age, our lives are deeply intertwined with technology. From online banking and shopping to personal communication and entertainment, we rely heavily on computers, smartphones, and the Internet. This increasing dependency makes understanding cybersecurity—protecting our electronic data—crucial for everyone. Here's a detailed exploration of why cybersecurity is so important, explained in simple terms.

The Rise of the Digital World

Imagine a world where nearly everything can be controlled at the touch of a button or the click of a mouse. Today, we live in such a world. We shop online, manage our bank accounts through apps, and share moments of our lives on social media. Even our homes, cars, and workplaces are connected to the internet, from smart thermostats to online project management tools.

As wonderful as this connectivity is, it opens up numerous doors for threats. Just as leaving your house or car unlocked could invite thieves, operating in a digital world without proper security measures can invite cybercriminals to steal, manipulate, or destroy your personal information.

Understanding the Stakes

Cybersecurity is about protecting that information. But what exactly are we protecting? Here are a few elements:

- **Personal Information**: This includes your name, address, emails, and more sensitive data like your social security number, bank account details, and medical records. If cybercriminals access this information, they could steal your identity, drain your bank accounts, or even blackmail you.

- **Business Data**: Companies hold not just their corporate secrets but also data about their employees and customers. A breach could lead to financial losses, legal consequences, and damage to the company's reputation.

- **National Security**: On the largest scale, cybersecurity protects a country's critical infrastructure, including the electricity grid, water purification systems, and transportation networks. Cyberattacks on these could lead to catastrophic consequences.

The Reality of Cyber Threats

Cyber threats come in various forms, and understanding these can help us appreciate the need for robust cybersecurity measures:

- **Viruses and Malware**: These are programs designed to infect your devices and spread to others, potentially harming files, stealing data, or both.

- **Phishing Attacks**: Here, attackers trick you into giving away personal information or downloading malware. This often involves emails or messages that appear to be from legitimate sources but are not.

- **Ransomware**: This type of malware locks you out of your files, with the attacker demanding payment to restore access. Even if you pay, there's no guarantee you'll regain access or that the attacker won't leave other malicious software on your device.

- **Data Breaches**: This occurs when cybercriminals break into a database to steal large quantities of personal or financial data. The repercussions can affect hundreds, thousands, or even millions of people.

Why Everyone Needs to Care

You might think, "Why would someone target me?" But cyber threats are often automated, scouring the internet for vulnerabilities without caring who the victims are. If your data is accessible and unprotected, it's at risk. Here's why everyone, not just big corporations or the technically savvy, should care about cybersecurity:

- **It Protects Individual Freedom**: Having personal information stolen can lead to a loss of privacy and autonomy. It can make you feel unsafe and violate your personal space.

- **Financial Health**: Cyber attacks can have direct financial impacts, from draining your bank account to impacting your credit score.

- **Trust in Digital Systems**: Strong cybersecurity practices build trust in the digital tools we use daily, from email to online banking. Without this trust, the digital economy could not function effectively.

Conclusion

In a world as interconnected as ours, the importance of cybersecurity cannot be overstated. It's not just about protecting bits of data; it's about protecting our way of life. By understanding the risks and taking appropriate measures to safeguard our information, we can all contribute to a safer digital environment. Whether it's choosing strong passwords, keeping our devices updated, or educating ourselves about potential scams, each step we take is a building block toward greater security.

THE EVOLUTION OF CYBERSECURITY

The concept of cybersecurity has evolved significantly over the years. From its origins in the simplistic safeguards of the past to the complex systems that protect our digital era, understanding this evolution helps us appreciate its critical role in our contemporary world.

1. The Genesis of Cybersecurity

Cybersecurity, in its earliest form, began as the practice of securing physical records and communications. Even ancient civilizations had methods to protect messages, such as the use of cyphers by the Greeks and Romans. However, the term "cybersecurity" truly found its relevance with the advent of computers and the internet.

2. The Rise of the Digital Age

As the digital age dawned, the need for robust cybersecurity became apparent. The introduction of the internet transformed how we share information, but it also introduced new vulnerabilities. Cyberattacks have become more sophisticated, targeting large organisations and individuals. This era saw the rise of viruses, malware, and network attacks, prompting an evolution in cybersecurity measures.

3. Cybersecurity Today

Today, cybersecurity is an integral part of IT infrastructure for governments, businesses, and individuals alike. It involves various practices and technologies to protect networks, computers, programs, and data from attack, damage, or unauthorized access.

4. Why Cybersecurity is Critical in the Modern Digital Era

In the modern digital era, almost every aspect of our lives is online or connected. This connectivity brings immense convenience and efficiencies but also significant risks. Personal, financial, and business data that traverse the internet can be prime targets for cybercriminals. Thus, cybersecurity is essential not only to protect individual privacy but also to safeguard national security, the economy, and the internet's infrastructure.

5. The Evolution of Cyber Threats

Cyber threats have evolved from simple viruses to sophisticated cyber espionage tools used by state actors. The scope and scale of cyberattacks have expanded dramatically, evidenced by incidents like the WannaCry ransomware attack, which affected hundreds of thousands of computers across the globe.

6. Future Challenges and Opportunities

As technology advances, so too do the tactics of cyber attackers. The future of cybersecurity lies in the development of more sophisticated defensive technologies such as artificial intelligence (AI) and machine learning (ML) to predict, detect, and respond to threats faster than ever before.

Conclusion

The history of cybersecurity is a testament to the ongoing battle between cyber defences and cyber threats. Its evolution is closely tied to the advancements in technology and the corresponding increase in cyber risks. As we look to the future, the importance of cybersecurity continues to grow, making it an essential pillar of the digital age.

In crafting this chapter, we are reminded of the ever-present need to advance our cybersecurity capabilities to protect our increasingly digital way of life. This chapter not only educates but also emphasizes the critical role cybersecurity plays in the modern world.

OVERVIEW OF CYBERSECURITY

In today's digital world, the significance of cybersecurity is more pronounced than ever. As we increasingly depend on digital technologies for daily activities, the need to protect our information systems from attack, damage, or unauthorized access becomes a critical priority. This overview aims to demystify cybersecurity by breaking it down into its core components, explaining its importance, and outlining the key areas that are protected by effective cybersecurity measures.

What is Cybersecurity?

Cybersecurity refers to the practice of defending computers, servers, mobile devices, electronic systems, networks, and data from malicious attacks. It is also known as information technology security or electronic information security. The term applies in a variety of contexts, from business to mobile computing, and can be divided into a few common categories:

1. **Network Security:** The process of protecting the network from unwanted users, attacks, and intrusions.

2. **Application Security:** Ensuring that applications are free of threats and vulnerabilities that could compromise them.

3. **Information Security:** Protecting the integrity and privacy of data, both in storage and in transit.

4. **Operational Security:** Involves the processes and decisions for handling and protecting data assets. This includes the permissions users have when accessing a network and the procedures that determine how and where data may be stored or shared.

5. **Disaster Recovery and Business Continuity:** Defining how an organization responds to cybersecurity incidents or any other event that causes the loss of operations or data. Disaster recovery policies dictate how the organization restores its operations and information to return to the same operating capacity as before the event. Business continuity is the plan the organization falls back on while trying to operate without certain resources.

6. **End-user Education:** Addressing the most unpredictable cybersecurity factor: people. Anyone can accidentally introduce a virus to an otherwise secure system by failing to follow good security practices. Teaching users to delete suspicious email attachments, not plug in unidentified USB drives, and various other important lessons is vital for the security of any organization.

Importance of Cybersecurity

Why is cybersecurity important? In today's connected world, everyone benefits from advanced cyber defence programs. At an individual level, a cybersecurity attack can result in everything from identity theft, to extortion attempts, to the loss of important data like family photos. Everyone relies on critical infrastructures like power plants, hospitals, and financial service companies. Securing these and other organizations is essential to keeping our society functioning.

Everyone also benefits from the work of cyber threat researchers, like the team at the National Cybersecurity and Communications Integration Center (NCCIC), who leverage their expertise to analyze and reduce cybersecurity risks.

Common Cybersecurity Threats

Understanding the enemy is the first step in cybersecurity. Here are some common cyber threats:

1. **Malware:** It's software that does malicious tasks on a device or network such as corrupting data or taking over a system.

2. **Phishing:** It's the practice of sending fraudulent emails that resemble emails from reputable sources. The aim is to steal sensitive data like credit card numbers and login information.

3. **Man-in-the-Middle (MitM) attacks:** This occurs when attackers insert themselves into a two-party transaction. After interrupting the traffic, they can filter and steal data.

4. **Denial-of-service attacks:** These attacks involve the flooding of systems, servers, or networks with traffic to exhaust resources and bandwidth. As a result, the system becomes unable to process and fulfil legitimate requests.

Cybersecurity Best Practices

To protect oneself from the increasing number of cyber threats, here are some best practices:

- Install reputable antivirus software and keep it updated.

- Use strong passwords. Consider using password management software to keep your passwords locked down.

- Keep your operating system, software, and applications updated.

- Be wary of suspicious emails and pop-ups.

- Back up your data regularly in case information is lost.

- Secure your network.

Conclusion

Cybersecurity is crucial for everyone, from individuals to large organizations, and even governments. The methods used to attack individuals and organizations evolve rapidly, and understanding these tactics is the first step in creating an effective shield against them. Protecting yourself and your organization from cyber threats requires awareness, education, and practical application of security tools and policies. Whether it's personal data or corporate security, a small investment in cybersecurity can go a long way toward preventing a catastrophic breach.

CHAPTER 1: UNDERSTANDING CYBER THREATS

Introduction

Imagine a world where every piece of digital information—from your social media details to top-secret government documents—is under constant threat. Cyber threats are sinister efforts by hackers and other malcontents aimed at stealing, destroying, or causing chaos in the digital sphere. As we dive into the murky waters of cyber threats, we uncover the strategies employed by these digital adversaries and the innovative defences we need to counteract them.

1. What Are Cyber Threats?

Cyber threats involve various harmful actions that aim to steal, damage, or mess with data digitally. These activities range from deploying harmful software, like viruses, to carrying out massive campaigns that paralyse websites. As our reliance on technology grows, so does the creativity of these digital villains, making it crucial to keep our cybersecurity game strong.

2. Current Cyber Threat Landscape

Let's talk numbers to understand the gravity of the situation:

- This year, we've seen a 30% jump in cyber attacks compared to the last.

- Ransomware incidents have climbed by 20%, with hackers locking files and demanding hefty ransoms.

- A whopping 80% of security incidents stem from cunning phishing scams.

3. Ransomware Attacks

Ransomware attacks remain a pervasive threat in 2024. Cybercriminals continue to refine their techniques, employing advanced encryption and targeted strategies. These attacks can paralyse organisations, leading to substantial financial losses and reputational damage.

- Employ advanced encryption and targeted strategies

- Cripple organisations and lead to significant financial losses and reputational damage

- Protect against ransomware through robust backup strategies, employee awareness training, and regular security patching

4. Phishing and Spear-Phishing

Imagine receiving an email that looks like it's from your bank, asking for your account details. That's phishing. Spear-phishing takes this a notch higher, targeting specific individuals with personalised traps. It's a significant threat, with over 90% of breaches initiated through such deceits.

5. Distributed Denial of Service (DDoS) Attacks

DDoS attacks flood websites with so much traffic that they collapse under the pressure. It's like a crowd of gatecrashers showing up at a party uninvited, only the party is your website, and it gets shut down.

6. Insider Threats

Sometimes the danger is from within. Insider threats arise from people inside the organisation—employees, and contractors—who have access to sensitive information. They account for about 34% of all data breaches.

7. Internet of Things (IoT) Vulnerabilities

With the proliferation of IoT devices, the attack surface for cybercriminals expands. In 2024, IoT vulnerabilities pose significant risks as many devices lack adequate security measures. Hackers can exploit these weaknesses to gain unauthorised access or launch distributed denial-of-service (DDoS) attacks.

- Expansion of the attack surface due to the proliferation of IoT devices

- Lack of adequate security measures in many IoT devices

- Mitigate IoT vulnerabilities by using strong passwords, regular firmware updates, and network segregation

8. Cloud Security Threats

As businesses flock to cloud computing for convenience, the bad guys see opportunities in misconfigurations and weak security practices. The result? A surge in breaches highlights the need for tighter cloud security measures.

9. Artificial Intelligence (AI) and Machine Learning (ML) as Threats

AI and ML are double-edged swords. While they help us build better security tools, they also empower cybercriminals to create smarter malware that can learn and adapt to our defences.

10. Advanced Persistent Threats (APTs)

APTs are sophisticated, long-term cyber-attacks targeting specific entities, such as governments or large organisations. In 2024, APTs continue to pose a grave threat, leveraging stealthy techniques to gain unauthorised access and maintain persistence within networks.

- Sophisticated, long-term cyber-attacks targeting specific entities

- Use stealthy techniques to gain unauthorised access and maintain persistence within networks

- Mitigate APTs through strong access controls, regular security assessments, and advanced threat detection and response technologies

Case Studies

Sony Pictures Entertainment Attack (2014): A high-profile cyberattack where attackers accessed and released confidential data, significantly impacting the company.

WannaCry Ransomware Attack (2017): A global cyber incident that affected hundreds of thousands of computers across 150 countries, highlighting the rapid spread and broad impact of ransomware.

Conclusion

Navigating the complex world of cyber threats requires more than just good software—it demands awareness, vigilance, and a proactive approach to cybersecurity. Understanding these threats and the measures to counter them equips us with the tools needed to defend our digital frontiers effectively. Let's keep learning and adapting to ensure our digital lives are secure and our data remains ours.

CYBER THREATS AND THEIR IMPACT ON GLOBAL BUSINESS OPERATIONS

In the rapidly advancing world of technology, cybersecurity remains a critical concern for businesses globally. As businesses continue to integrate digital solutions into their operations, the landscape of cyber threats also evolves, becoming more sophisticated and potentially more damaging. This comprehensive overview explores the dynamic nature of cyber threats and their significant impacts on global business operations.

Understanding Cyber Threats

Cyber threats are malicious activities that seek to damage data, steal data, or disrupt digital life in general. Cyber attacks can lead to significant financial, reputational, and operational damage to businesses and governments. To fully grasp the impact of these threats, it's important to understand their diverse forms and how they have evolved.

Common Types of Cyber Threats:

1. **Malware:** This is malicious software, including viruses and ransomware, that gets installed on a machine or network. Once installed, malware can block access to key components of the network, covertly obtain information by transmitting data from the hard drive, or disrupt certain components and render the system inoperable.

2. **Phishing:** These attacks use fraudulent communication, typically an email, that appears to come from a legitimate source. The goal is to steal sensitive data like credit card and login information or to install malware on the victim's machine.

3. **Man-in-the-Middle (MitM) Attacks:** These occur when attackers intercept an existing conversation or data transfer. After inserting themselves in the "middle" of the transfer, the attackers can impersonate the parties, steal data, or manipulate the communication.

4. **Denial-of-Service (DoS) and Distributed Denial-of-Service (DDoS) Attacks:** These attacks aim to overwhelm systems, servers, or networks with traffic to exhaust resources and bandwidth. As a result, the system is unable to process legitimate requests.

5. **Advanced Persistent Threats (APTs):** These are prolonged targeted attacks where attackers infiltrate a network to steal information over a long period without being detected.

6. **Cryptojacking:** This is the unauthorized use of someone else's computer to mine cryptocurrency. Hackers do this by either getting the victim to click on a malicious link in an email that loads crypto mining code on the computer, or by infecting a website or online ad with JavaScript code that auto-executes once loaded in the victim's browser.

The Evolution of Cyber Threats

The nature of cyber threats has evolved significantly as technology has advanced. Early viruses and worms were primarily designed to damage systems or gain bragging rights. Today, cyber threats are more sophisticated and stealthy, designed to steal huge amounts of data or cause significant financial and reputational damage to organizations.

For instance, ransomware attacks have evolved to a point where they are now aimed at specific businesses with the ability to pay large ransom. Phishing tactics have also become more sophisticated, using social engineering to tailor messages that are much harder for users to identify as malicious.

Impact on Global Business Operations

The impact of cyber threats on global business operations can be severe and multifaceted. Here's how:

1. **Financial Loss:** From theft of corporate information, disruption in trading, and the cost of repairing damaged systems, cyber threats can drain a company's financial resources.

2. **Reputation Damage:** Cyber attacks can damage a company's reputation and erode the trust that customers have in their products or services. This is especially damaging for brands that promise data privacy and security as part of their value proposition.

3. **Operational Disruption:** Many businesses experience operational disruption as a result of cyber-attacks which can result in loss of business and reduced operational capacity.

4. **Regulatory Consequences:** Businesses in many sectors are subject to regulatory requirements around data security. Cyber attacks that compromise customer data can lead to regulatory fines and sanctions.

5. **Intellectual Property Loss:** Companies in the technology and creative industries often fall victim to cyber-attacks aimed at stealing intellectual property to gain a competitive advantage.

6. **Strategic Business Decisions:** The threat of cyber attacks affects decisions at the highest levels of a company. Executives must balance the focus on innovation and growth with the necessity for securing assets and data.

Conclusion

The evolving landscape of cyber threats presents a persistent challenge to global business operations. As these threats continue to grow in complexity and sophistication, businesses must enhance their cybersecurity measures and remain vigilant against potential cyber-attacks. This involves not only investing in technology to protect themselves but also training employees to recognize threats and respond effectively. A comprehensive approach to cybersecurity is essential for protecting businesses against the ever-changing threat landscape and securing their future in the digital age.

UNDERSTANDING ATTACK VECTORS AND THEIR GLOBAL IMPLICATIONS

Imagine living in a city where every window, door, and alleyway could potentially let a thief into your home. In the digital world, attack vectors are like these windows and doors. They are the pathways that hackers use to sneak into systems, steal stuff, and sometimes just cause trouble. This detailed exploration dives into what these attack vectors are, how they work, and the ripple effects they have around our globe. It's like understanding the cracks in our digital walls so we can patch them up properly.

1. What Are Attack Vectors?

Explaining the Basics:

- **Attack Vector:** Think of it as a sneaky path or tool that a cyber thief uses to break into your digital house.

- **Purpose:** These are used to access, steal, or destroy data—or sometimes, to take control of whole systems.

- **Common Types:** Phishing (tricking you into giving up secrets), malware (software designed to harm), ransomware (locking your files unless you pay up), and many others.

Grasping these concepts is key to building better locks on our digital doors—that's why understanding attack vectors is crucial for anyone using technology today.

2. Common Attack Vectors

Phishing Attacks: Fishing for Secrets

- **How It Works:** You receive an email that looks real—it might say it's from your bank or a friend—but it's fake. You click a link, and just like that, they've got your secrets.

- **Impact:** People lose money, businesses lose data, and trust in digital communication takes a hit.

Malware: The Hidden Bugs

- **What's Going On:** Malware is bad software that sneaks into your computer, from viruses that spread like a cold, to spyware that watches your every move.

- **Impact:** It can steal your info, erase your data, or turn your computer into a zombie soldier in a hacker army.

Ransomware: Digital Kidnapping

- **Scenario:** Imagine someone locks up all your digital files, even your precious photos, and won't give them back unless you pay a ransom. That's ransomware.

- **Impact:** It's costly, and it's scary because anyone's data can be locked up at any time.

Distributed Denial of Service (DDoS): The Digital Traffic Jam

- **How It Happens:** Imagine a road so packed with cars that nobody can move—that's what a DDoS attack does to websites. It floods them with so much fake traffic that they can't function.

- **Impact:** Websites go down, businesses can't operate, and the digital economy suffers.

3. Global Implications of Attack Vectors

Economic Implications: Money Matters

- **The Costs:** Cybercrime costs the world billions of dollars—not just in stolen money but in fixing the damages and securing systems.

- **Business Impact:** Companies spend a lot on cybersecurity, driving up the costs of their products and services.

Social Implications: Trust Issues

- **Public Trust:** With each attack, people become more wary of using digital services, which can slow down the progress of digital innovation.

- **Privacy Fears:** Everyone starts worrying more about their info, wondering if it's truly safe.

Political Implications: Beyond Borders

- **Election Security:** Hacking can influence elections by spreading misinformation or even altering vote counts.

- **International Tensions:** Cyberattacks can strain relationships between countries, especially if they suspect one another of spying or sabotage.

4. Fighting Back: How to Mitigate Attack Vectors

Education and Training: Knowledge as a Shield

- **Employee Training:** Teach staff to spot phishing emails and use strong passwords.

- **Public Awareness:** Campaigns to inform the public about how to stay safe online.

Technology Upgrades: Building Better Defenses

- **Regular Updates:** Keep software up-to-date to protect against new threats.

- **Advanced Security Tools:** Firewalls, antivirus software, and more sophisticated defences to guard against complex attacks.

Policies and Regulations: Setting Digital Rules

- **Stronger Laws:** Governments implement strict cybersecurity laws to protect people and businesses.

- **International Cooperation:** Countries working together to fight cybercrime across borders.

Conclusion

Just like a city with better roads, lights, and locks is safer, a digital world with strong cybersecurity is safer for everyone. Understanding attack vectors and their global implications is not just about stopping hackers; it's about building a resilient digital society. By fortifying our digital spaces, educating our people, and cooperating globally, we can safeguard our collective digital future.

CHAPTER 2: PERSONAL CYBERSECURITY

In today's digital era, every swipe, click, and tap connects us more deeply into a vast digital landscape, but also opens doors to potential digital threats. Whether it's your social media account or bank details, understanding how to shield your digital presence is more crucial than ever. This guide dives into simple yet effective strategies to fortify your cybersecurity, ensuring your digital life remains private and protected.

1. Grasping the Basics of Personal Cybersecurity

Essentials to Know:

- **Personal Cybersecurity:** It's all about keeping your private information safe from unauthorized snooping or damage.

- **Scope:** This includes everything from your social media interactions to the financial details saved on your phone or computer.

Every digital user's first defence is knowing what needs protection—identifying what's at risk sets the stage for building strong defences.

2. Keeping Your Software Up-to-Date

Simple Steps for Big Protection:

- **Routine Updates:** Regular updates patch security holes that could let hackers in. Keep your operating systems and apps up to date.

- **Automatic Updates:** Turn on automatic updates wherever possible; it's the easiest way to stay ahead of threats.

- **Mobile Updates:** Don't forget your mobile devices—they are as vulnerable as your computer.

Software updates are like renewing the locks on your doors as thieves invent new ways to pick them.

3. Crafting Strong, Unique Passwords

Creating Barriers:

- **Strong Passwords:** Mix letters, numbers, and symbols, and make them long. Think of them as long passwords, not just complex ones.

- **Unique Passwords:** Use a different password for every account. It's like using a different key for every door.

- **Password Managers:** These apps create and remember complex passwords for you, requiring you to remember just one master password.

Passwords are your first line of defence; make them strong and varied.

4. Enabling Multi-Factor Authentication (MFA)

An Extra Layer of Security:

- **How It Works:** MFA requires you to verify your identity in two or more ways—something you know (like a password) plus something you have (like a code sent to your phone).

- **Activation:** Turn on MFA for all important accounts, especially email, banking, and social media.

MFA is like adding a deadbolt to your already locked door.

5. Staying Alert Against Phishing

Spotting the Hooks:

- **Recognising Phishing:** Be sceptical of emails or messages pressing for immediate action or asking for personal information.

- **Verification:** If a message seems off, contact the organisation through an official number or website, not through the provided links.

Phishing tries to trick you into opening your door to thieves. Know the signs to keep it closed.

6. Securing Your Home Network

Your Digital Fort:

- **Router Settings:** Change default usernames and passwords.

- **Encryption:** Use the strongest encryption setting available, preferably WPA3.

- **Disable Unnecessary Features:** Turn off features like Remote Management to minimise vulnerabilities.

Your home network is the gateway to your digital home. Secure it.

7. Protecting Your Mobile Devices

On-the-Go Security:

- **Screen Locks:** Always use a PIN, password, or biometric option to lock your phone.

- **Device Tracking:** Activate features like 'Find My iPhone' or Android's 'Find My Device'.

- **App Permissions:** Only grant necessary permissions to apps, and regularly review what access they have.

- **Software Updates:** Install updates promptly to protect against vulnerabilities.

- **Securing Mobile Transactions:** Use secure networks for transactions, avoid public Wi-Fi for financial operations, and consider using VPNs.

Mobile devices are your digital keys; keep them safe and under your control.

8. Backing Up Your Data

Your Safety Net:

- **Automated Backups:** Use cloud services or external drives for automatic backup settings.

- **Backup Testing:** Regularly check that you can recover files from your backups—just to be sure.

Backups are your insurance policy against digital disasters.

9. Keeping Informed

Staying Ahead:

- **Educational Resources:** Follow reputable cybersecurity blogs, podcasts, and news outlets.

- **Training and Workshops:** Engage in any available cybersecurity training to stay sharp and informed.

Knowledge is power, especially when it comes to cybersecurity.

Conclusion

Mastering personal cybersecurity isn't just about protecting data—it's about securing your gateway to the digital world. With the right knowledge and tools, you can keep your digital life both vibrant and secure. Stay vigilant, stay updated, and remember, the best defence is a good offence.

ADVANCED PERSONAL SECURITY PRACTICES FOR IT PROFESSIONALS

In the world of bytes and bits, IT professionals stand as the guardians and role models of cybersecurity. It's not just about fighting off cyber threats but also about setting a strong example within their organizations. This guide goes deep into advanced personal security practices that IT professionals should adopt and teach to ensure both their safety and that of their teams.

1. The Power of Example: Modeling Best Practices

Role Model Influence:

- **Position of Trust:** IT professionals access sensitive data and systems, placing them in a uniquely influential position.

- **Setting the Standard:** Their adherence to security protocols can inspire and establish security norms within the team.

By embodying the best cybersecurity practices, IT professionals can lead by example, encouraging their teams to mirror these protective behaviours, thereby fortifying the organisation's digital defences.

2. Championing Multi-Factor Authentication (MFA)

Building a Fortified Entry Point:

- **Layered Security:** MFA adds extra security layers, making unauthorised access considerably more difficult.

- **Education and Advocacy:** It's crucial for IT pros to not only implement MFA but also explain its value and operation to their teams.

- **Real-world Applications:** Demonstrating how MFA blocks unauthorised access through real-life scenarios can underline its importance.

MFA is like a multi-lock system on your digital doors, significantly enhancing your security posture.

3. Mastery of Encryption

Safeguarding Data Privacy:

- **Encryption Standards:** Use and understand high-standard encryption methods like AES to protect data privacy.

- **Practical Training:** Regular sessions to educate teams on how encryption protects data, particularly data in transit and at rest.

- **Protocol Implementation:** Ensuring all data exchanges over the network are secured through protocols like HTTPS and SSH.

Encryption is the art of turning legible data into a coded message that only the right key can decode.

4. Network Defense Strategies

Securing the Digital Perimeter:

- **Defensive Tools:** Utilize firewalls and antivirus solutions to shield against malicious attacks.

- **Vigilant Monitoring:** Keep a constant watch on network traffic to spot and address unusual activities swiftly.

- **Encouraging VPN Use:** Promote using Virtual Private Networks to ensure secure remote access.

Effective network security acts as a robust barrier, protecting against intrusions and threats.

5. Proactive Security Assessments

Staying Ahead of Threats:

- **Routine Audits:** Regular security checks to gauge the organization's security health.

- **Ethical Hacking:** Hiring ethical hackers for penetration testing to identify and rectify vulnerabilities.

- **Learning from Tests:** Use insights from tests to fortify defences and train the team against common security lapses.

Regular assessments help you spot cracks in your digital fortress so you can patch them before intruders slip through.

6. Diligent Data Management and Privacy

Ensuring Compliance and Trust:

- **Policy Development:** Craft comprehensive data management and privacy policies that align with laws like GDPR or HIPAA.

- **Education on Data Handling:** Continuously train staff on proper data handling procedures to prevent leaks and breaches.

Data is a valuable asset that needs stringent rules and careful handling to maintain its confidentiality and integrity.

7. Efficient Incident Response

Minimising Damage:

Response Team Formation: Build a team ready to tackle various security incidents.

- **Drill Simulations:** Regularly simulate potential security breaches to test response efficacy.

- **Strategy Refinement:** Continuously improve strategies based on drill feedback and real incident learnings.

A swift and effective incident response can drastically reduce the potential damage from security breaches.

8. Continuous Learning and Awareness

Keeping Pace with Cyber Trends:

- **Staying Informed:** Regular updates on the latest in cybersecurity help anticipate and mitigate new threats.

- **Engaging Workshops:** Lead and participate in workshops and seminars to enhance the team's skills and knowledge.

The cybersecurity landscape is ever-changing, and staying informed is crucial to defending against novel threats.

Conclusion

For IT professionals, mastering personal cybersecurity practices isn't just about self-protection; it's about leadership and education. By adopting and demonstrating these advanced practices, they not only protect their domains but also cultivate a culture of security awareness and preparedness that is evident throughout the organisation. This proactive approach is vital in building a resilient defence against the evolving landscape of cyber threats.

CHAPTER 3: PASSWORDS AND AUTHENTICATION

In the realm of cybersecurity, passwords function as the first line of defence against unauthorized access to personal and organizational data. A strong password can significantly reduce the risk of security breaches by making it challenging for attackers to gain access. This detailed guide will explain how to create strong passwords and why it's important to protect your digital identity.

1. Introduction to Password Security

Passwords are a fundamental aspect of information security. They are used to authenticate users by confirming their identity through something they know. However, not all passwords provide equal security. Simple and commonly used passwords can be easily guessed or cracked by attackers using various methods. Thus, understanding how to create strong passwords is essential for anyone who uses online services.

2. What Makes a Password Strong?

A strong password is hard to guess and difficult for breach attempts via automated software. Here are the key characteristics of a strong password:

- **Length:** The more characters a password has, the more combinations an attacker has to try before guessing it correctly. A minimum of 12 characters is recommended.

- **Complexity:** A mixture of uppercase letters, lowercase letters, numbers, and special characters (such as ! @, #, $) increases complexity.

- **Unpredictability:** Avoid common words, phrases, or predictable patterns (like "password123" or "qwerty").

3. The Risk of Weak Passwords

Weak passwords pose significant risks:

- **Ease of Cracking:** Simple passwords can be quickly cracked using brute-force methods, where every possible password combination is tested until the correct one is found.

- **Vulnerability to Common Attacks:** Techniques such as dictionary attacks, where attackers use common words and phrases to break into accounts, are effective against weak passwords.

- **Account Compromise:** Once an attacker has cracked a password, they gain access to personal information and may commit identity theft, financial fraud, or other malicious activities.

4. Tips for Creating Strong Passwords

Creating a strong password that you can also remember might seem daunting, but it's manageable with the right techniques:

- **Use a Passphrase:** Consider using a passphrase made up of several words that are easy for you to remember but hard for others to guess. An example could be a combination of three unrelated words like "CoffeeDeskRain."

- **Incorporate Complexity:** Add complexity by deliberately misspelling words, incorporating numbers, and using special characters. For instance, "C0ff33D3sk!Ra!n".

- **Personalize Securely:** Make your password unique to you but avoid using easily accessible information such as birthdays, anniversaries, or names.

- **Use Acronyms:** Create an acronym from a sentence that's meaningful to you. For example, "I love to play basketball at 5 PM on Saturdays!" can be turned into "Il2pb@5Pm0S!"

5. Using Password Managers

Remembering a unique, strong password for each account can be challenging. Password managers can help:

- **Store Passwords Securely:** Password managers store your passwords in a securely encrypted vault.

- **Generate Strong Passwords:** They can generate strong, random passwords for you, that you don't need to remember.

- **Auto-fill Passwords:** They can auto-fill passwords on login pages, so you don't need to type them.

6. Best Practices in Password Management

To enhance password security further, consider these best practices:

- **Regularly Update Passwords:** Change your passwords regularly to limit breaches. Every three to six months is a good standard.

- **Avoid Reusing Passwords:** Each account should have a unique password. Reusing passwords across multiple sites increases the risk if one site is compromised.

- **Enable Multi-factor Authentication (MFA):** MFA adds a layer of security by requiring additional verification (like a code sent to your phone) to access your account.

Conclusion

In today's digital world, the importance of strong passwords cannot be overstated. By following the guidelines outlined in this document, you can significantly enhance your cybersecurity posture. Remember, protecting your digital accounts with strong, unique passwords is a crucial step in safeguarding your personal information against potential cyber threats.

EXPLORATION OF BIOMETRIC AND MULTI-FACTOR AUTHENTICATION METHODS

In our digital world, keeping sensitive information secure is a top priority for both individuals and organizations. The use of traditional passwords is now being boosted by more advanced methods like biometric and multi-factor authentication (MFA). This guide will take you through these methods in a way that's easy to understand and apply.

Introduction to Authentication Methods

Authentication is just a fancy word for checking if someone has the right to access something. It's like verifying a person's ticket before letting them into a concert. In digital terms, this usually starts with passwords or PINs—something only the user should know.

Understanding Biometric Authentication

What is Biometric Authentication?

Biometric authentication is a techy way of using parts of your body, like fingerprints or your face, to prove who you are. Here's how it works:

- **Data Capture:** A device scans your unique feature, like your thumbprint.

- **Data Storage:** This fingerprint is then turned into digital data and saved in a system.

- **Comparison:** Next time you need to prove it's you, the device scans you again and checks if the new scan matches the saved one.

Benefits of Biometric Authentication:

- **Increased Security:** It's tough to copy someone's fingerprint or face, making this a secure method.

- **Ease of Use:** Forget about remembering passwords—just use your finger.

- **Quick Authentication:** It's fast. Just a look or a touch can unlock access.

But, it's not perfect.

- **Privacy Concerns:** Storing personal traits like fingerprints could lead to privacy issues if the data gets into the wrong hands.

- **Potential Errors:** Sometimes, the system might not recognise you due to minor changes or errors, denying access or letting the wrong person in.

- **Cost:** Setting up these systems can be expensive and complex.

What is Multi-Factor Authentication (MFA)?

Multi-factor Authentication (MFA) means using more than one method to verify it's you. Think of it as needing both a key and a fingerprint to open a treasure chest.

Types of Authentication Factors:

- **Something You Know:** Like a password or a PIN.

- **Something You Have:** This could be a security token or an app on your phone.

- **Something You Are:** This includes biometrics, like your fingerprints or face.

How MFA Works:

- **Layered Defense:** By asking for more than one proof of identity, MFA makes it much harder for someone to sneak in.

- **Step-by-Step Verification:** For example, you might enter a password and then have to confirm a code on your phone.

Benefits of MFA:

- **Enhanced Security:** Adding extra hurdles can significantly improve security.

- **Flexibility:** Companies can customize MFA to fit their needs.

- **Reduced Phishing Risks:** Even if someone steals your password, they won't easily get past a second security layer.

But there are challenges:

- **Inconvenience:** It can feel like a hassle, especially if it takes time.

- **Costs:** MFA systems can be pricey to set up and maintain.

- **Device Dependence:** Lose your phone, and you might lose access.

- **Tutorial:** Using Password Managers Effectively

What is a Password Manager?

A password manager is like a digital vault that keeps all your passwords locked away safely. You only need to remember one master password to access them all.

How to Use a Password Manager:

- **Choose a Password Manager:** Options like LastPass, Dashlane, and 1Password are popular.

- **Set It Up:** Install the app and create a strong master password. This is the only password you need to remember!

- **Add Your Passwords:** You can enter them manually or let the manager save them as you log into sites.

- **Use It Daily:** Whenever you visit a site, your password manager will offer to fill in your password for you.

Comparing Popular Options:

- **LastPass:** Great for beginners with a user-friendly interface.

- **Dashlane:** Offers extra features like dark web monitoring.

- **1Password:** Best for those who want advanced security options.

Conclusion

Biometric and multi-factor authentication are great steps forward in keeping our digital lives secure. They offer better protection than old-school passwords. However, they also bring new challenges, especially around privacy and costs. As technology evolves, we'll continue to see new ways to keep our data safe. Always choose the method that balances security with convenience for your needs.

CHAPTER 4: NETWORK SECURITY BASICS

In our increasingly digital world, securing our networks at home and in small offices has never been more crucial. Network security is all about keeping your internet-connected systems safe from various cyber threats. This guide will take you through the basics of setting up a secure home and small office network, offering practical examples and recommendations for routers and network tools that enhance security.

Understanding Network Security

What is Network Security?

It's the shields and armour that protect the integrity, confidentiality, and accessibility of your computer networks and data. It involves a mix of hardware and software technologies designed to fend off cyber threats that are becoming more common by the day.

Setting Up a Secure Home Network

What is a Home Network?

It's your digital ecosystem. This network connects your home devices—like computers, smartphones, tablets, and even your gaming consoles and smart home devices—to the internet. Most home networks today are wireless, which brings convenience but also potential security risks.

Common Home Network Vulnerabilities:

- **Weak Encryption:** Poor encryption allows attackers to eavesdrop on your data.

- **Default Settings:** Failing to change the default settings on routers and devices makes it easier for attackers to break in.

- **Unsecured Devices:** Many devices, especially IoT devices like smart thermostats and cameras, come with minimal security protections.

How to Secure Your Home Network:

• **Change Default Credentials:** Replace factory usernames and passwords with strong, unique ones.

• **Use Strong Encryption:** Activate WPA3 encryption on your Wi-Fi network. If that's not available, use WPA2.

• **Regularly Update Firmware:** Ensure your router and any connected devices are always running the latest software to protect against vulnerabilities.

• **Enable Network Firewalls:** Most modern routers come with built-in firewalls. Make sure this feature is turned on.

Recommended Routers for Enhanced Security:

• **Netgear Nighthawk:** Known for robust security features and strong performance.

• **Google Nest Wi-Fi:** Offers built-in security tools and easy management through an app.

Setting Up a Secure Small Office Network

What is an organisation network?

It's the backbone that connects all of an organisation's devices and facilitates data and resource sharing. Office networks are usually more complex than home setups and require additional security layers to protect sensitive business information.

Common Vulnerabilities in Small Office Networks:

• **Insider Threats:** Sometimes, the danger comes from within, with employees accidentally or intentionally leaking data.

• **Outdated Systems:** Not updating your systems can leave doors open for cybercriminals.

• **Phishing Attacks:** Staff can be deceived into giving away sensitive info or downloading harmful software.

How to Secure Your Small Office Network:

- **Implement Strong Access Controls:** Limit network access to employees who need it.

- **Conduct Regular Security Audits:** Use penetration testing to find and fix vulnerabilities.

- **Educate Employees:** Teach your team about security risks like phishing and how to avoid them.

- **Use Advanced Threat Protection:** Tools like intrusion detection systems (IDS) and endpoint detection and response (EDR) can help spot and stop attacks.

Recommended Network Tools for Enhanced Security:

- **Cisco Meraki MX:** Offers comprehensive threat management and is ideal for small to medium-sized businesses.

- **Ubiquiti UniFi Security Gateway:** Provides advanced firewall policies and persistent threat management to protect your network.

Best Practices for Network Security

- **Regular Updates:** Keep all systems and software patched with the latest security updates.

- **Secure Configuration:** Set up your systems and devices to close any unused ports and disable services you don't use.

- **Backup Data:** Regularly back up important data and ensure you can restore it if needed. Always test your backup procedures.

- **Multi-factor Authentication (MFA):** Always use MFA to add an extra layer of security, requiring more than just a password to access sensitive systems.

Conclusion

By understanding network security basics and implementing strong protective measures, you can keep your home and office networks safe from cyber threats. As these threats evolve, so should your strategies to stay secure, ensuring a resilient and reliable digital environment for both personal and professional use.

LATEST TECHNOLOGIES AND ARCHITECTURES IN NETWORK SECURITY

In today's digital age, as the number of internet-connected devices skyrockets, the sophistication of cyber threats also escalates. It's crucial to stay updated with the latest advancements in network security to protect our networks effectively. This guide will introduce you to the cutting-edge technologies and architectures currently shaping the field of network security, using simple language and practical examples.

Introduction to Modern Network Security

What is Modern Network Security?

Modern network security is a fortress comprising various defences like hardware, software, and smart strategies designed to protect the networks that connect and run our digital lives. It needs to be dynamic, ready to adapt to emerging threats and protect a vast digital landscape.

Advanced Network Security Technologies

1. Cloud-based security (SecaaS)

Think of cloud-based security as hiring a team of security guards who work remotely. These services, from antivirus applications to comprehensive security operations, are delivered over the internet and tailored to fit any size of organisation.

Advantages:

- **Cost-Effective:** Generally cheaper than traditional methods.

- **Scalability:** Easily adjusts to the size of the business.

- **Ease of Updates:** Enhancements and updates are handled by the provider, ensuring you're always covered by the latest defences.

Challenges:

- **Dependency on the Internet:** Your security is only as good as your Internet connection.

- **Privacy Concerns:** Storing sensitive data off-site can lead to concerns about who else might access it.

2. Artificial Intelligence (AI) and Machine Learning (ML)

AI and ML in network security are like having a super-smart detective who can predict where the next attack will come from. These technologies analyze mountains of data to spot patterns and predict potential breaches before they happen.

Use Cases:

- **Automated Threat Detection:** Identifying threats without human help.

- **Predictive Analytics:** Using past data to predict future breaches.

Implications:

- **Resource Intensive:** Requires significant processing power.

- **Complexity:** May be difficult to integrate and manage within existing systems.

3. Blockchain Technology

Blockchain is best known for its role in cryptocurrency, but it's also a robust security tool. Its decentralised nature and immutable records make it nearly impossible to alter data without authorisation.

Applications:

- **Secure Transactions:** Ensures that transactions are secure and verifiable.

- **Identity Verification:** Provides a robust method for verifying identities online.

Limitations:

- **Resource Intensive:** Consumes a significant amount of computational power.

- **Integration Challenges:** Difficult to integrate with existing systems.

Emerging Network Security Architectures

1. Zero Trust Architecture

Zero Trust operates on a simple principle: trust no one. It assumes that threats could be both outside and inside the network, so it verifies everything trying to connect before access is granted.

Features:

- **Microsegmentation:** Divides the network into smaller, manageable zones, each requiring separate verification.

- **Least Privilege Access:** Users are given only the access necessary to perform their tasks.

Benefits:

- **Reduced Attack Surface:** Limits the opportunities for attackers.

- **Enhanced Data Security:** Helps protect sensitive data by limiting access.

2. Software-defined perimeter (SDP)

SDP makes a network's infrastructure invisible. It creates direct connections between the user and the resources they need, which are not accessible to anyone else.

Advantages:

- **Reduced Visibility:** By making resources invisible, it lessens the chances of attacks.

Considerations:

- **Complex Implementation:** Switching from traditional security models to SDP can be challenging.

Integration of IoT Security

With the rapid growth of IoT devices, from refrigerators to fitness trackers, securing these devices has become a priority. IoT security is about safeguarding connected devices and the networks they operate on.

Technologies:

- **IoT Security Platforms:** These systems manage device security from a central point, simplifying the protection of a diverse array of devices.

Challenges:

- **Device Diversity:** Many IoT devices have poor built-in security, making them vulnerable to attacks.

- **Constant Monitoring:** IoT devices require ongoing surveillance to keep them secure.

Conclusion

As the landscape of digital threats evolves, so too must our strategies for defending against them. By embracing the latest technologies and architectures in network security, organisations and individuals can significantly enhance their defence mechanisms. Keeping abreast of these advancements and adapting to new solutions are crucial for maintaining robust network security in our interconnected world. By understanding and implementing these advanced solutions, we can ensure that our digital environments are secure and resilient against the myriad of cyber risks we face today.

CHAPTER 5: PROTECTING YOUR ONLINE IDENTITY

In today's world, where social media platforms are central to both our personal and professional lives, understanding how to protect our online identities is crucial. This comprehensive guide explores the risks associated with social media and provides effective strategies for safeguarding your online presence at both personal and corporate levels.

Understanding Online Identity

What is an Online Identity?

Your online identity is essentially how you appear on the internet. It includes your social media profiles, email addresses, and any personal information that's publicly available online. Protecting this identity is vital to avoid identity theft, fraud, and other online risks.

Risks of Social Media

Social media isn't just about connecting with friends or promoting your business; it also comes with several risks that can jeopardize your safety and privacy.

1. Privacy Leaks

- **What Happens:** Personal information shared on social media can be easily accessed by hackers and used for malicious purposes.

- **Consequence:** Over-sharing can lead to identity theft.

2. Phishing and Scams

- **How It Works:** Users may receive messages that seem to be from legitimate sources but aim to steal sensitive information.

- **Risk:** Social media scams can lure users into giving away personal information or money.

3. Cyberbullying and Harassment

- **Impact:** Social media can facilitate cyberbullying and harassment, affecting mental health and well-being.

4. Fake Profiles and Catfishing

- **Concern:** Imposters create fake profiles to deceive, manipulate, or exploit users, often leading to emotional or financial harm.

Protecting Personal Online Identities

How to Maintain a Secure Online Presence:

1. Privacy Settings

- **Action:** Adjust your privacy settings on social media to control who sees your posts and personal information.

- **Tip:** Regularly review and update these settings to stay current with platform changes.

2. Mindful Sharing

- **Best Practice:** Be cautious about posting personal details like addresses, phone numbers, and family information.

- **Safety Tip:** Avoid sharing location details or daily routines that could put you at risk.

3. Strong Passwords and Authentication

- **Security Measure:** Use strong, unique passwords for each of your social media accounts.

- **Enhanced Security:** Enable multi-factor authentication wherever possible to add an extra layer of protection.

4. Education on Phishing and Scams

- **Knowledge is Power:** Learn to recognize phishing attempts and too-good-to-be-true offers.

- **Preventive Action:** Report and block suspicious accounts and messages.

Protecting Corporate Online Identities

For businesses, managing social media is critical due to its power as a marketing tool and its potential security risks.

1. Social Media Policies

- **Policy Development:** Create clear guidelines that define acceptable behaviours and security practices for employees.

- **Coverage:** Policies should address sharing confidential company information and proper online representation.

2. Employee Training

- **Training Programs:** Regularly educate employees on securing their personal and professional social media accounts.

- **Focus Areas:** Include training on recognizing and mitigating social media-based threats.

3. Monitoring and Responding

- **Active Monitoring:** Keep an eye on social media for unauthorized use of your brand and fake profiles.

- **Crisis Management:** Establish protocols for quickly addressing social media crises, whether they involve information breaches or PR issues.

Regular Audits and Reviews

Maintaining Security:

- **Routine Checks:** Regularly audit your social media security practices and review policies.

- **Access Control:** Ensure that only authorized personnel have access to edit and manage social media accounts.

Legal Considerations

Compliance and Law:

- **Legal Compliance:** Ensure your social media activities align with privacy laws and regulations.

- **Awareness:** Stay informed about the legal implications of your online actions.

Conclusion

Securing your online identity on social media requires continuous vigilance, smart practices, and ongoing education. By implementing robust security measures and staying aware of potential risks, both individuals and businesses can enjoy the benefits of social media without compromising their safety or privacy. This proactive approach will help you maintain a strong and secure online presence in our interconnected digital world.

MANAGING DIGITAL FOOTPRINTS AND MITIGATING RISKS

In our interconnected digital era, every click, post, and login leaves a mark—your digital footprint. This trail paints a detailed picture of your online behaviour and preferences, which can be beneficial but also pose substantial risks. This guide delves into managing your digital footprints effectively and provides strategies to safeguard your privacy and security online.

Understanding Digital Footprints

What is a Digital Footprint?

A digital footprint consists of the data trail left by your interactions online. It includes:

- **Active Footprints:** Actions like emails you send, social media comments, and online articles you publish.

- **Passive Footprints:** Data collected without your direct action, often through cookies, which log details like your IP address, device type, and browsing habits.

Risks Associated with Digital Footprints

Neglecting to manage your digital footprints can expose you to several risks:

- **Privacy Loss:** Personal details can become accessible to strangers, leading to potential stalking or harassment.

- **Identity Theft:** Exposure of sensitive data such as addresses and banking details can lead to identity theft.

- **Reputation Damage:** Inappropriate or offensive content can damage both personal and professional reputations.

- **Targeted Attacks:** Cybercriminals might use detailed personal information to craft sophisticated phishing schemes.

Strategies for Managing Digital Footprints

Be Selective About Sharing Information:

- **Think Before You Share:** Consider the potential impact of posting information. Be particularly cautious with sensitive details.

- **Use Privacy Settings:** Employ privacy controls on social media and other online platforms to manage who sees your information.

Regularly Review Online Accounts:

- **Audit Social Media:** Periodically go through your social media profiles to clean up old posts that may not reflect your current stance or that contain outdated personal information.

- **Check Privacy Policies:** Keep updated with how websites and apps are using your data by reviewing their policies regularly.

Mitigating Risks Associated with Digital Footprints

Secure Your Accounts:

- **Strong Passwords:** Create complex, unique passwords for different accounts.

- **Two-Factor Authentication (2FA):** Enhance account security with 2FA, which requires a second form of identification beyond your password.

Be Cautious with Public Wi-Fi:

Use VPNs: A Virtual Private Network (VPN) encrypts your internet connection on public Wi-Fi, protecting your data from potential eavesdroppers.

Manage Cookies and Browsing Data:

- **Clear Cookies Regularly:** This helps reduce the buildup of data about your online activities.

- **Adjust Browser Settings:** Limit tracking by configuring your web browser's privacy settings and using private browsing modes when possible.

Educating Others About Digital Footprints

Raise Awareness:

- **Family and Friends:** Educate your loved ones about the importance of digital footprints and how to manage them responsibly.

- **Workplace:** Conduct training sessions for employees to emphasize the importance of data privacy and managing digital trails.

Using Technology to Manage Digital Footprints

Leverage Tools and Extensions:

- **Digital Footprint Management Tools:** Use these tools to monitor and control your online presence effectively.

- **Ad-Blockers and Privacy Extensions:** Install these on your browsers to reduce tracking and protect your privacy.

Interactive Scenarios: Avoiding Common Online Scams

Scenario 1: The Too-Good-To-Be-True Job Offer

- **Situation:** You receive an email offering a high-salary job with minimal requirements.

- **Red Flags:** Unprofessional email domain, spelling errors, and a payment request.

- **Safe Action:** Verify the company's legitimacy by checking its official website and contact details. Never share personal information or make payments based on unsolicited emails.

Scenario 2: The Urgent Charity Donation Request

•**Situation:** A message urges you to donate to a charity following a recent disaster.

•**Red Flags:** High-pressure tactics and vague details about how the funds are used.

•**Safe Action:** Research the charity on reputable sites like Charity Navigator before donating. Use official channels to make contributions.

Conclusion

Managing your digital footprint is more than a precaution; it's a necessity in today's digital world. By being mindful of the information you share, regularly updating your security measures, and educating those around you, you can protect your online identity from a myriad of threats. As digital landscapes evolve, so should your strategies to stay safe online.

CHAPTER 6: INTRODUCTION TO ENCRYPTION

Encryption is like a secret code that keeps your information safe from prying eyes. In today's digital world, where information travels at the speed of light across the internet, it's crucial to protect sensitive data. Whether it's personal emails, important financial documents, or private conversations, encryption helps ensure that only the intended recipient can read your messages. This guide dives into the basics of encryption, explores different techniques, and offers practical applications for everyday use.

1. Understanding Encryption

What is Encryption?

Encryption transforms readable data (plaintext) into a coded form (ciphertext) that only authorised parties can decode. It's like sending a locked chest where the recipient has the key.

2. How Does Encryption Work?

- **Encryption Process:** You start with the data you want to secure. This data is transformed using an algorithm and a key to create encrypted data.

- **Decryption Process:** The recipient uses a key to decode the encrypted data back into its original form.

3. Types of Encryption

There are two main types of encryption methods: symmetric and asymmetric.

Symmetric Encryption

In symmetric encryption, the same key is used for both encryption and decryption. Think of it like a locked box where both sender and recipient have the same key. It's fast and suitable for large volumes of data but requires secure key management practices since sharing the key can be risky.

Asymmetric Encryption

Asymmetric encryption, or public key encryption, involves two keys: a public key, which anyone can have, and a private key, which is kept secret by the owner. Messages are encrypted with the recipient's public key and can only be decrypted by their private key. This method is highly secure for communication over unsecured channels because the private key never needs to be shared.

4. Importance of Encryption

Encryption plays a critical role in securing data and communication, particularly in areas such as:

Data Security

Encryption ensures that sensitive data, whether stored on computers or transmitted across the internet, is secured against unauthorized access. This is crucial for personal data protection, corporate secrets, and government classified information.

E-commerce

When you shop online, encryption protects your financial and personal information as it travels between your computer and the e-commerce site's servers, making online shopping safer.

Email and Communication

Encryption secures emails and other forms of digital communication, ensuring that only the intended recipient can view the content, which protects against eavesdropping and unauthorized access.

Regulatory Compliance

Many industries have regulations that require data to be encrypted to protect sensitive information. This includes healthcare data under HIPAA, credit card information under PCI DSS, and personal data under GDPR.

5. Challenges in Encryption

While encryption is a powerful tool for security, it comes with challenges:

- **Complexity in Management:** Managing keys, especially in large organizations or systems that use encryption extensively, can be complex and resource-intensive.

- **Performance:** Encryption can slow down system performance because it requires additional processing to encrypt and decrypt data.

- **Encryption Breaks:** As technology evolves, older encryption methods can become vulnerable. Continuous updates and monitoring are required to ensure data remains secure.

6. Practical Applications of Encryption

Encrypting Personal Emails

- **Why It Matters:** To protect the privacy of your communications from being read by unauthorized entities.

- **How to Do It:** Use email services that provide end-to-end encryption or install encryption plugins.

Encrypting Personal Files

- **Why It Matters:** To secure your sensitive documents, especially if your device is lost or stolen.

- **How to Do It:** Use file encryption tools that integrate with your operating system or third-party encryption software.

Interactive Scenarios: Encryption in Action

Scenario 1: Encrypting an Email

Situation: You need to send your tax documents to your accountant via email.

Steps to Encrypt:

• Compose your email and attach your tax documents.

• Use an email service with built-in encryption or an encryption plugin.

• Verify that encryption is enabled and send the email securely.

• **Outcome:** Your accountant receives the email, decrypts the attachment with a key, and your sensitive information remains protected.

Scenario 2: Encrypting a Personal File

Situation: You want to store your medical records on your laptop.

Steps to Encrypt:

• Locate the file on your computer.

• Right-click on the file and select the option to encrypt.

• Enter a strong password when prompted.

• **Outcome:** Your medical records are encrypted and safe from unauthorised access, even if your laptop is stolen.

Managing and Reviewing Your Digital Footprint

Why It's Important:

- **Personal Security:** Keeping your digital footprint small and secure prevents identity theft.

- **Privacy:** Minimizes exposure to data breaches and unwanted surveillance.

How to Manage Your Digital Footprint:

- **Review and Audit:** Regularly check your online accounts and delete or encrypt sensitive information.

- **Limit Sharing:** Be cautious about what personal information you share online, especially on social media.

Conclusion

In conclusion, encryption is an essential security practice that protects data and maintains privacy in digital communications. By converting sensitive information into unreadable text, encryption helps to ensure that data remains confidential and secure from unauthorised access. Whether for personal use, business communications, or compliance with privacy laws, understanding and implementing strong encryption practices is crucial for anyone looking to secure their digital information.

ADVANCED ENCRYPTION TECHNIQUES AND THE EMERGING FIELD OF QUANTUM ENCRYPTION

In today's digital world, the demand for more robust and sophisticated encryption methods is rising. This is particularly crucial as we gear up for the future of quantum computing, which has the potential to transform the field significantly, while also presenting significant obstacles to current encryption methods. This detailed explanation delves into advanced encryption approaches and the emerging field of quantum encryption.

1. Advanced Encryption Techniques

Advanced encryption techniques are designed to provide stronger security for data by using complex algorithms and larger key sizes. These techniques ensure that data remains secure even as computing power increases and as cyber threats become more sophisticated.

AES (Advanced Encryption Standard)

One of the most widely used encryption standards today is AES. It's known for its speed and security, which makes it suitable for many applications, from securing online transactions to top-secret government communications. AES uses key sizes of 128, 192, or 256 bits, with AES-256 being the strongest.

RSA (Rivest–Shamir–Adleman)

RSA is one of the earliest forms of public-key cryptography and is widely used for secure data transmission. Unlike AES, it uses a pair of keys—a public encryption key, and a private decryption key. The strength of RSA encryption increases with the size of the key, but it is generally slower than AES and is used mainly for small data transfers or for encrypting the transmission of AES keys.

ECC (Elliptic Curve Cryptography)

ECC is another form of public-key cryptography that uses the algebraic structure of elliptic curves over finite fields. The advantage of ECC is that it offers the same level of security as RSA but with much smaller keys. Smaller keys result in faster operations and lower processing power requirements, making ECC particularly well-suited for mobile devices.

2. Quantum Encryption

Quantum encryption, also known as quantum cryptography, refers to using the principles of quantum mechanics to secure data in a way that is theoretically tamper-proof.

Quantum Key Distribution (QKD)

The most well-known application of quantum encryption is Quantum Key Distribution. QKD uses quantum mechanics to produce and distribute cryptographic keys securely. The unique property of QKD is that if an attempt is made to intercept the key, it changes the quantum state of the key, making the interception detectable. This allows the sender and receiver to be aware of any eavesdropping attempt, ensuring the ultimate security in key distribution.

Post-Quantum Cryptography (PQC)

With the advent of quantum computing, there is a growing need for cryptographic systems that are secure against both quantum and classical computers. Post-quantum cryptography aims to develop cryptographic systems that are secure against potential future quantum computers but can be implemented on classical computer systems as we know them today.

3. Implications of Quantum Computing on Encryption

Quantum computing poses a significant threat to traditional encryption methods. Quantum computers, once fully operational, could potentially break much of the encryption that currently secures our digital communications. This is because quantum computers can solve certain computational problems, such as factoring large numbers, which are the basis for many encryption methods, much faster than classical computers.

4. The Need for Quantum-Resistant Encryption

In response to the threat posed by quantum computing, researchers are actively developing quantum-resistant encryption methods. These methods aim to be secure against both classical and quantum computing attacks, ensuring that data remains protected even as quantum computing becomes more prevalent.

CHAPTER 7: CYBERSECURITY AT WORK

In our increasingly digital world, the importance of cybersecurity in the workplace cannot be overstated. As businesses rely more on technology for their operations, the potential for cyber threats increases. This guide explores how to establish effective cybersecurity practices to protect sensitive information and maintain business integrity.

1. Understanding the Need for Cybersecurity at Work

Cybersecurity involves protecting systems, networks, and programs from digital attacks. These cyber-attacks are usually aimed at accessing, changing, or destroying sensitive information; extorting money from users; or interrupting normal business processes. Implementing effective cybersecurity measures is challenging because there are more devices than people, and attackers are becoming more innovative.

2. Assessing Risks

Before implementing security measures, it's crucial to understand and assess the potential risks:

- **Risk Assessment:** Identify what data needs protection and understand the repercussions of a breach. This involves understanding what information is most sensitive or vital to your company's operations.

- **Threat Analysis:** Consider the types of cyber threats your business may face, such as ransomware, phishing, or data breaches. This analysis helps tailor the cybersecurity measures to be more effective.

3. Establishing a Cybersecurity Policy

A clear and comprehensive cybersecurity policy is essential for any business. This policy should outline:

- **Employee Responsibilities:** Define what is expected from employees regarding cybersecurity. This includes safe browsing habits, the use of strong passwords, and the handling of sensitive information.

- **Response Strategies:** Provide guidelines on how to respond to different types of cyber threats and data breaches.

- **Regular Updates:** Ensure the policy is updated regularly to adapt to new cybersecurity challenges and threats.

4. Implementing Strong Cybersecurity Measures

Several technical and procedural measures must be implemented to ensure strong cybersecurity in the workplace:

- **Use of Firewalls and Antivirus Software:** Firewalls act as barriers between your network and potential threats, while antivirus software helps to detect and eliminate malicious software.

- **Data Encryption:** Encrypt sensitive data both in transit and at rest to protect it from unauthorized access.

- **Multi-factor Authentication (MFA):** Implement MFA wherever possible to add an extra layer of security, making it harder for attackers to gain access to devices and networks.

- **Secure Wi-Fi Networks:** Make sure that your company's Wi-Fi network is secure, encrypted, and hidden. Use strong passwords and consider using a VPN.

5. Training Employees

Educating your workforce is one of the most cost-effective cybersecurity measures you can implement:

- **Regular Training Sessions:** Conduct regular training to keep employees aware of the latest cybersecurity threats and practices.

- **Phishing Simulations:** Regularly simulate phishing attacks to teach employees how to recognize and handle suspicious emails.

- **Best Practices:** Educate employees on the importance of strong passwords, the dangers of using public Wi-Fi, and the proper use of company devices.

6. Monitoring and Response

Constant monitoring of company networks and systems is crucial for early detection of potential security breaches:

- **Monitoring Tools:** Use monitoring tools to keep an eye on network traffic and unusual activities.

- **Incident Response Plan:** Develop a robust incident response plan that outlines what steps to take when a cybersecurity incident occurs. This plan should include notifying customers and regulatory bodies if necessary.

- **Regular Audits:** Conduct audits of your cybersecurity practices to ensure they are effective and to identify any vulnerabilities that need to be addressed.

7. Maintaining Compliance

Depending on your industry, there may be regulatory requirements governing data security that your business needs to comply with:

- **Understand Compliance Requirements:** Be aware of any legal or regulatory requirements for protecting data in your sector.

- **Implement Compliance Measures:** Ensure your cybersecurity practices meet all required regulations to avoid legal penalties and breaches of trust.

Case Studies: Success Stories in Cybersecurity Implementation

1. **A Tech Startup Enhances Security Measures:**

- **Challenge:** Vulnerable to data breaches due to inadequate security protocols.

- **Solution:** Implemented comprehensive MFA, regular employee training, and advanced threat detection systems.

- **Outcome:** Significantly reduced the incidence of security breaches and enhanced overall trust with clients.

2. **A Retail Company Battles Phishing Attacks:**

- **Challenge:** Employees are frequently targeted by phishing scams, risking sensitive customer data.

- **Solution:** Introduced phishing simulations and intensive security awareness programs.

- **Outcome:** Employees became adept at recognising scams, nearly eliminating successful phishing attacks.

Conclusion

Cybersecurity is a crucial factor in running a modern business. To safeguard themselves from various cyber threats, companies should evaluate risks, establish comprehensive policies, implement robust security measures, educate their employees, and ensure compliance. Maintaining strong cybersecurity practices not only protects your business but also your customers, helping to maintain trust and credibility in the digital age.

BUILDING A SECURITY-FIRST CORPORATE CULTURE AND EFFECTIVE SECURITY TRAINING STRATEGIES

In today's world, digital security threats are constantly present. Therefore, it is crucial to promote a security-first corporate culture to protect a company's digital assets. This guide provides a comprehensive plan to create such a culture and implement effective security training. This way, every employee can become capable of defending the organisation's cybersecurity.

1. Understanding a Security-First Corporate Culture

1. What is a Security-First Culture?

In a security-first culture, cybersecurity is not just the responsibility of the IT department; it's a fundamental aspect of every employee's role. Security is considered in every business decision and every aspect of daily operations.

2. Characteristics of a Security-First Culture:

- **Proactive Approach to Security:** Anticipating potential threats and addressing them proactively.

- **Regular Communication:** Consistent discussion about cybersecurity across all levels of the organisation, ensuring it remains a focal point.

- **Empowerment and Responsibility:** Each employee feels accountable for the security of information, empowered to act to protect the company.

2. Leadership and Commitment

Role of Leadership in Cultivating Security Awareness:

- **Top-Down Commitment:** Leadership must prioritize and demonstrate their commitment to cybersecurity, influencing the entire organisation's mindset.

- **Resource Allocation:** Committing necessary resources—including budget and personnel —to support cybersecurity initiatives.

- **Visible Support:** Leaders should actively participate in cybersecurity efforts, showing their support and integrating security into business strategy.

3. Integrating Security Into Business Processes

Embedding Security in Daily Operations:

- **Security by Design:** Integrating security considerations at the beginning of all project planning phases, not as an add-on.

- **Risk Management Integration:** Including cybersecurity risks in the company's overall risk management plans.

- **Policy Development and Enforcement:** Creating and enforcing robust security policies that support both security and business objectives.

4. Effective Security Training Strategies

Training Employees to be Security-Savvy:

- **Comprehensive Training Programs:** Regular, mandatory training that includes everything from basic security practices to advanced threat detection.

- **Role-Specific Training:** Tailoring training to the specific needs of different departments to ensure relevance and effectiveness.

- **Engaging Training Techniques:** Employing interactive methods like gamification and simulations to enhance engagement and retention.

5. Building Awareness and Vigilance

Maintaining Ongoing Cybersecurity Awareness:

- **Regular Updates:** Keeping staff informed about emerging threats and new security practices through regular communications.

- **Security Champions:** Designating knowledgeable advocates within departments to promote security best practices and serve as go-to resources.

- **Encouraging Incident Reporting:** Developing a culture that supports reporting security issues without fear of negative repercussions.

6. Evaluating and Improving Security Practices

Continuous Improvement in Cybersecurity Practices:

- **Feedback Mechanisms:** Encouraging feedback on security practices from employees at all levels to identify areas for improvement.

- **Regular Security Audits:** Conducting thorough audits and assessments to identify vulnerabilities and assess the effectiveness of current security measures.

- **Adaptability:** Remaining flexible to adapt training and policies in response to evolving cybersecurity landscapes.

Conclusion

Developing a corporate culture that prioritizes security is a crucial strategy that requires commitment from all levels of an organisation. By creating an environment where cybersecurity is given importance and continually improved, businesses can not only protect themselves against current threats but also increase their ability to withstand future challenges. This cultural shift is essential for organizations looking to safeguard their valuable digital assets in today's threat-rich digital landscape.

CHAPTER 8: AI AND MACHINE LEARNING IN CYBERSECURITY

Artificial Intelligence (AI) and Machine Learning (ML) are revolutionising how we tackle cybersecurity, transforming the way we protect against and respond to cyber threats. This guide provides a layman-friendly introduction to AI and ML, highlighting how these technologies enhance cybersecurity efforts with real-world examples.

1. What are AI and Machine Learning?

Artificial Intelligence (AI):

AI refers to the capability of machines to perform tasks that typically require human intelligence. This includes complex functions like recognising speech, interpreting complex data, making decisions, and solving problems.

Machine Learning (ML):

ML is a subset of AI focused on the ability of machines to learn from data, recognise patterns, and make decisions with minimal human input. Over time, ML systems improve and adapt without needing explicit reprogramming.

2. AI and ML in Cybersecurity

Enhancing Cyber Defenses with AI and ML:

Threat Detection:

- **Real-Time Monitoring:** AI systems can monitor network activities continuously, detecting unusual behaviour that could signal a cyber threat.

- **Behavioural Analysis:** ML algorithms learn to identify what normal behaviour looks like for a network and can spot unusual patterns that may indicate a breach.

Threat Intelligence:

- **Automated Intelligence Gathering:** AI automates the collection and analysis of data about emerging threats, helping cybersecurity teams stay ahead of new challenges.

- **Predictive Analysis:** ML can analyze past data to predict potential future attacks, allowing preemptive action.

Vulnerability Management:

- **Automated Patching:** AI systems can manage the application of software patches to vulnerabilities, ensuring that systems are up-to-date and less vulnerable to attacks.

- **Vulnerability Scanning:** ML algorithms can efficiently scan systems for weaknesses, learning over time to better identify security gaps.

3. Real-world examples of AI in Cybersecurity

Case Study 1: AI-Driven Threat Detection System

A large financial institution implemented an AI system to monitor their network traffic. The system was designed to detect anomalies in real time, such as unexpected data transfers or unauthorized access attempts. This proactive approach allowed the company to quickly isolate and mitigate threats before they caused significant damage.

Case Study 2: ML-Powered Behavioral Analysis

An e-commerce company used ML to understand typical user behaviours on their platform. The system flagged unusual transactions and login patterns, which helped prevent a series of attempted frauds by detecting them as they happened.

4. Benefits of AI and ML in Cybersecurity

- **Scalability:** AI and ML systems can handle increasing volumes of data and security events more efficiently than human teams.

- **Accuracy:** These technologies minimize human errors and increase the precision of threat detection and responses.

- **Cost-Effectiveness:** Over time, AI and ML can reduce costs by automating routine tasks, allowing human resources to focus on strategic activities.

5. Challenges and Considerations

- **Complex Training Needs:** AI and ML systems require extensive data and sophisticated algorithms, which need continuous updates to cope with evolving cyber threats.

- **Privacy Issues:** The use of AI in cybersecurity can lead to privacy concerns, as these systems often process sensitive data.

- **Over-reliance Risk:** Dependence on automated systems can be problematic if those systems fail, highlighting the need for human oversight.

Conclusion

Artificial Intelligence (AI) and Machine Learning (ML) are powerful tools that are transforming the field of cybersecurity. They can improve threat detection and automate responses, providing significant advantages in safeguarding digital environments. However, it is essential to implement them thoughtfully while considering the technological and ethical challenges they pose. This approach can help organisations bolster their cybersecurity measures and establish a more secure and resilient digital infrastructure.

USE OF PREDICTIVE ANALYTICS FOR THREAT DETECTION AND RESPONSE

Predictive analytics in cybersecurity involves using data, statistical algorithms, and machine learning techniques to identify the likelihood of future events based on historical data. This approach is increasingly crucial in cybersecurity for anticipating, detecting, and responding to potential threats before they cause harm. This detailed explanation explores how predictive analytics is applied in cybersecurity, enhanced by case studies to illustrate its practical uses.

1. Understanding Predictive Analytics in Cybersecurity

Predictive analytics helps cybersecurity professionals manage emerging threats by analyzing trends and patterns from past cyber incidents. This analysis can predict where vulnerabilities and attacks are most likely to occur, allowing organizations to strengthen their defences proactively.

Key Components of Predictive Analytics:

- **Data Collection:** Gathering vast amounts of data from various sources within the organization, including network traffic, logs, past security incidents, and external threat intelligence.

- **Data Analysis:** Using statistical tools and algorithms to analyze the collected data, identify patterns, and make predictions.

- **Machine Learning Models:** Employing machine learning to refine predictions over time, learning from new data and outcomes to improve accuracy.

2. Applications in Threat Detection and Response

Predictive analytics can transform how organisations approach cybersecurity in several ways:

Anticipating Attacks

By analyzing patterns that lead up to a security breach, predictive analytics can identify the likelihood of similar incidents occurring. This allows cybersecurity teams to implement specific countermeasures preemptively.

Prioritising Threats

Not all security alerts are created equal. Predictive analytics helps in distinguishing between false alarms and serious threats by evaluating the risk associated with each alert. This enables security professionals to focus their efforts where they are needed most.

Optimizing Resource Allocation

Predictive insights can guide decisions about where to allocate security resources more effectively, ensuring that the most vulnerable areas receive the most attention.

3. Case Studies

To illustrate the effectiveness of predictive analytics in cybersecurity, let's consider a few case studies:

Case Study 1: Banking Sector

- **Situation:** A major bank was experiencing frequent phishing attacks that compromised customer accounts.

- **Action:** The bank implemented predictive analytics to analyze the attributes of emails and user behaviours that typically led to successful phishing attacks.

- **Outcome:** The predictive models could identify suspicious email patterns and flag them before reaching customer inboxes, significantly reducing phishing success rates.

Case Study 2: E-commerce Platform

- **Situation:** An e-commerce company struggled with credit card fraud, which was escalating rapidly due to the high volume of transactions.

- **Action:** The company used predictive analytics to assess the risk of fraud associated with each transaction in real-time, based on previous purchasing patterns, customer details, and common characteristics of fraudulent purchases.

- **Outcome:** This approach allowed the company to prevent a substantial percentage of potential fraud, saving millions in potential losses.

4. Challenges in Using Predictive Analytics

While predictive analytics offers significant benefits, it also comes with challenges:

- **Data Quality and Quantity:** Effective predictive analytics requires high-quality and extensive data, which can be difficult to collect and manage.

- **Skill Requirements:** Analyzing data and developing predictive models require specialised skills in data science and machine learning, which may necessitate significant training or hiring.

- **Constant Evolution:** Cyber threats continually evolve, meaning predictive models must be regularly updated and retrained to remain effective.

Conclusion

Predictive analytics represents a powerful tool in the cybersecurity arsenal, offering the ability to not just react to threats, but anticipate and prevent them. By understanding and implementing predictive analytics, organisations can enhance their security posture significantly—staying one step ahead of cybercriminals. As shown in the case studies, whether it's banking or e-commerce, predictive analytics can provide actionable insights that protect business assets and customer data from emerging cyber threats.

CHAPTER 9: ENTERPRISE CYBERSECURITY

Enterprise cybersecurity is crucial for protecting the information and assets of large organizations from digital threats. This involves a comprehensive approach that encompasses various strategies, tools, and practices designed to secure network systems, data, and applications from cyber-attacks. An essential component of this is implementing effective risk management frameworks and strategies. This guide will break down the basics of risk management in enterprise cybersecurity.

1. Understanding Enterprise Cybersecurity

Enterprise cybersecurity refers to the collective measures, technologies, and processes that an organization uses to protect its digital assets from unauthorized access, attacks, or data theft. The goal is to ensure the confidentiality, integrity, and availability of the organization's data and IT infrastructure.

2. Risk Management in Cybersecurity

Risk management in cybersecurity is the process of identifying, analyzing, and mitigating risks associated with the organization's network and information assets. It is a fundamental aspect that helps protect an enterprise from potential cyber threats and reduces the impact should a breach occur.

Key Elements of Risk Management

- **Risk Identification:** The first step is identifying potential risks that could affect the organization. This includes threats to digital assets like data breaches, malware infections, system outages, and more.

- **Risk Assessment:** Once risks are identified, the next step is to assess their likelihood and potential impact. This helps in prioritizing which risks need immediate attention and which can be monitored over time.

- **Risk Mitigation:** Developing strategies to manage and mitigate the identified risks. This includes implementing security measures, choosing security technologies, and developing policies and procedures.

3. Risk Management Frameworks

A risk management framework provides a structured approach to managing the uncertainties related to digital assets. Here are some widely recognised frameworks:

NIST Cybersecurity Framework

Developed by the **National Institute of Standards and Technology**, this framework is popular globally for its comprehensive approach to managing cybersecurity risk. It comprises five core functions: Identify, Protect, Detect, Respond, and Recover.

- **Identify:** Develop an organizational understanding to manage cybersecurity risk to systems, assets, data, and capabilities.

- **Protect:** Implement appropriate safeguards to ensure critical infrastructure services.

- **Detect:** Implement appropriate activities to identify the occurrence of a cybersecurity event.

- **Respond:** Take action regarding a detected cybersecurity event.

- **Recover:** Maintain plans for resilience and restore any capabilities or services that were impaired due to a cybersecurity event.

ISO 27001

ISO 27001 is an international standard that provides specifications for an information security management system (ISMS). It helps organizations secure their information systematically and cost-effectively, through the adoption of an Information Security Management System (ISMS).

COBIT

COBIT (Control Objectives for Information and Related Technologies) is a framework for IT management and IT governance. It is a supportive tool that allows managers to bridge the gap between control requirements, technical issues, and business risks.

4. Implementing a Risk Management Strategy

Implementing an effective risk management strategy involves several steps:

- **Regular Audits and Assessments:** Conduct regular security audits to assess the effectiveness of current security measures. This helps in identifying vulnerabilities that need to be addressed.

- **Employee Training and Awareness:** Employees often represent the first line of defence against cyber threats. Regular training sessions on the latest security threats and best practices are essential.

- **Incident Response Plan:** Develop and maintain an incident response plan that outlines what to do in the event of a cyber attack. This should include roles and responsibilities, communication plans, and recovery steps.

- **Continuous Improvement:** Cybersecurity is not a one-time effort but a continuous process. Regularly review and update security measures and policies to adapt to new threats.

Conclusion

Effective risk management in enterprise cybersecurity involves understanding potential risks, assessing their impact, and developing strategies to mitigate them. By adopting robust risk management frameworks such as NIST, ISO 27001, or COBIT, organizations can enhance their security postures and protect themselves against the evolving landscape of cyber threats. These frameworks provide a systematic approach to managing cybersecurity risks that are crucial for safeguarding an enterprise's digital assets.

EXPLORATION OF ENTERPRISE SECURITY SOLUTIONS

Enterprise security is a critical concern for organizations looking to protect their digital assets from cyber threats. This comprehensive guide delves into key security technologies—Intrusion Detection Systems (IDS) and Intrusion Prevention Systems (IPS)—and explores advanced security solutions like Zero Trust architectures and Security Information and Event Management (SIEM) systems. We'll also look at real-world examples of security planning and incident handling, including lessons learned from major security breaches.

1. Understanding IDS and IPS

Intrusion Detection Systems (IDS) and Intrusion Prevention Systems (IPS) are fundamental components of network security that detect and prevent cyber threats respectively.

Intrusion Detection Systems (IDS)

• **What is IDS?** IDS are tools that monitor network traffic to detect suspicious activity and potential threats. They alert system administrators when such activities are detected.

• **Types of IDS:**

  • Network-based IDS (NIDS) monitors traffic on the entire network.

  • Host-based IDS (HIDS) monitors a single host for suspicious activity.

Intrusion Prevention Systems (IPS)

• **What is IPS?** IPS extends IDS capabilities by not only detecting threats but also taking action to prevent the threat from causing harm.

• **Functionality:** IPS can block traffic from a suspicious source, quarantine infected systems, and even correct cyclic redundancy check (CRC) errors in traffic.

2. Zero Trust Architectures

Zero Trust is a security concept centred on the belief that organizations should not automatically trust anything inside or outside its perimeters and instead must verify anything and everything trying to connect to its systems before granting access.

Principles of Zero Trust:

• **Least Privilege Access:** Limit user access with just enough access and just-in-time access.

- **Microsegmentation:** Breaks up security perimeters into small zones to maintain separate access for separate parts of the network.

- **Multi-factor Authentication (MFA):** Requires multiple methods of verification to gain access to resources.

3. Security Information and Event Management (SIEM) Systems

SIEM systems provide a holistic view of an organization's information security, combining SIM (Security Information Management) and SEM (Security Event Management) to provide real-time analysis of security alerts generated by applications and network hardware.

Functions of SIEM:

- **Data Aggregation:** Gathers data from multiple sources.

- **Event Correlation:** Links related records to identify patterns that might indicate a potential threat.

- **Alerting:** Notifies administrators about potential security issues.

- **Dashboards:** Tools to visualize and analyze data.

4. Real-world examples of Enterprise Security Planning and Incident Handling

Case Study: A Financial Institution Implements IDS/IPS

- **Scenario:** A bank faced repeated attempts of data breaches.

- **Action:** Deployed NIDS to monitor network traffic and HIDS on critical servers, supplemented by an IPS to actively block malicious activities.

- **Outcome:** The institution saw a significant reduction in unauthorized access attempts.

Case Study: Retail Company Adopts Zero Trust

- **Scenario:** A large retailer suffered a massive data breach, losing sensitive customer data.

- **Action:** Implemented a Zero Trust architecture, requiring MFA and re-evaluating all access privileges.

- **Outcome:** Enhanced security posture with a substantial decrease in incidents of data loss.

5. Lessons Learned from Major Security Breaches

- **Notable Breach:** Equifax

- **Lesson:** Outdated systems and unpatched vulnerabilities can lead to disastrous breaches. Regular updates and patches are essential.

- **Response:** Equifax stepped up efforts in monitoring its network and implementing stricter access controls.

Notable Breach: Sony

- **Lesson:** Lack of adequate security measures and slow response can aggravate the situation. Quick and efficient incident response is crucial.

- **Response:** Sony enhanced its cybersecurity infrastructure by integrating advanced IDS/IPS and employing real-time SIEM solutions.

Conclusion

Modern enterprises require robust security solutions to protect against sophisticated cyber threats. Technologies like IDS, IPS, Zero Trust architectures, and SIEM systems are critical components of an effective cybersecurity strategy. By learning from past security breaches and implementing advanced security measures, organizations can significantly enhance their resilience against cyber threats. Implementing these technologies and practices requires careful planning, execution, and ongoing management to ensure that they remain effective over time.

UNDERSTANDING CLOUD SECURITY:

Many small to medium-sized businesses are utilising cloud computing to improve their efficiency, reduce costs, and expand their operations in today's digital landscape. Nonetheless, the adoption of cloud technologies necessitates the implementation of strong cloud security measures. This guide aims to provide a comprehensive overview of cloud security by examining its challenges and best practices, with a particular emphasis on solutions designed for SMEs.

1. What is Cloud Security?

Cloud security is a collection of procedures, technologies, policies, and controls employed to protect cloud-based systems, data, and infrastructure. From authenticating access to filtering traffic, cloud security can be configured to the exact needs of the business.

2. Challenges of Cloud Security

Data Breaches:

- **Issue:** Perhaps the most pressing concern in cloud security is the risk of data breaches. A breach can expose sensitive customer information, intellectual property, and other valuable data to unauthorized parties.

- **Implication:** Such breaches not only lead to financial losses but can also damage a company's reputation and customer trust irreparably.

Data Loss:

- **Issue:** Data loss can occur due to malicious attacks, accidental deletion by users, or catastrophic failures in the cloud infrastructure.

- **Implication:** Losing critical data can disrupt business operations and lead to significant operational and financial setbacks.

Insufficient Identity, Credential, and Access Management:

- **Challenge:** Ensuring that only authorised users have access to specific levels of data and services in the cloud is a complex issue. Poor identity and access management can provide an easy entry point for attackers.

- **Risk:** Inadequate credential management can lead to unauthorised access and misuse of the cloud environment.

Insecure Interfaces and APIs:

- **Challenge:** Cloud service providers expose a set of software interfaces or APIs that customers use to manage and interact with cloud services. These interfaces must be securely designed to prevent unauthorised access and data breaches.

- **Concern:** Vulnerabilities in APIs can lead to unauthorised access and data exposure.

Account Hijacking:

- **Issue:** Phishing, fraud, and software exploits are still effective techniques for cybercriminals to hijack user accounts.

- **Consequence:** Once a user's account is compromised, attackers can manipulate data, eavesdrop on transactions, and redirect clients to illegitimate sites.

Lack of Visibility and Control:

- **Challenge:** Cloud environments inherently limit visibility and control over data and operations. Not seeing or controlling where your data resides or who accesses it can complicate security efforts.

- **Result:** This lack of transparency can make it difficult to detect security breaches on time.

Shared Technology Vulnerabilities:

- **Challenge:** In cloud computing, infrastructure, platforms, and applications are shared by multiple users. A vulnerability in one component can affect the security of the entire environment.

- **Implication:** Shared technology can amplify the impact of a single attack, affecting multiple tenants of the shared infrastructure.

Compliance Challenges:

- **Issue:** Meeting regulatory compliance requirements is more complex in the cloud where data storage, processing, and management might cross multiple international jurisdictions.

- **Complexity:** Ensuring compliance with standards such as GDPR, HIPAA, or PCI DSS becomes more complicated when data is distributed across various cloud services.

3. Best Practices for Cloud Security in SMEs

Strong Access Control:

- **Practice:** Implement robust authentication mechanisms, such as multi-factor authentication (MFA), to enhance security.
- **Benefit:** Reduces the risk of unauthorized access.

Data Encryption:

- **Application:** Encrypt data at rest and in transit to protect sensitive information from interception and breaches.
- **Advantage:** Ensures data confidentiality and integrity.

Regular Security Assessments:

- **Need:** Conduct regular audits and security assessments to identify and address vulnerabilities.
- **Outcome:** Helps in maintaining a secure cloud environment and compliance with relevant regulations.

Employee Training:

- **Importance:** Train employees on cloud security best practices and the importance of using secure and complex passwords.
- **Effect:** Increases security awareness and reduces the risk of human errors leading to security incidents.

Backup and Recovery Procedures:

- **Strategy:** Implement automated backups and have a clear disaster recovery plan in place.
- **Purpose:** Ensures business continuity in case of data loss or a major cybersecurity incident.

Use of Managed Security Services:

- **Option:** Consider using managed security services from reputable providers to help manage cloud security.

- **Suitability:** Particularly beneficial for SMEs with limited in-house IT resources

4. Cloud Security Solutions for AWS, Google Cloud, and Azure

Amazon Web Services (AWS):

AWS Identity and Access Management (IAM):

- **Solution:** Manage user access and encryption keys. AWS IAM allows you to set user permissions and policies to ensure that only authorized and authenticated users can access your resources.

- **Benefit:** Enhances security by ensuring that rights and privileges are adequately managed.

Amazon Cognito:

- **Solution:** Provides user sign-up, sign-in, and access control to web and mobile apps quickly and easily.

- **Benefit:** Secures user access on a large scale.

AWS Shield:

- **Solution:** Provides managed Distributed Denial of Service (DDoS) protection.

- **Benefit:** Safeguards applications running on AWS without the need for the user to engage in complex configurations.

Google Cloud Platform (GCP):

Google Cloud Identity & Access Management:

- **Solution:** Manages access control by defining who (identity) has what access (roles) to resources hosted in Google Cloud.

- **Benefit:** Ensures that only authorised users and services can access specific resources, reducing the risk of data breaches.

Google Cloud Armor:

- **Solution:** Provides DDoS defence and web application firewall (WAF) capabilities to protect applications and websites.

- **Benefit:** Enhances security against multiple types of attacks on the internet.

Google Virtual Private Cloud (VPC):

- **Solution:** Offers a private network with IP allocation, routing, and network firewall policies to securely run code.

- **Benefit:** Provides a secure and isolated environment for your cloud resources.

Microsoft Azure:

Azure Active Directory (Azure AD):

- **Solution:** Provides identity services that support multifactor authentication, conditional access policies, and single sign-on (SSO).

- **Benefit:** Strengthens security by ensuring only authorized users can access environments and applications.

Azure Security Center:

- **Solution:** Unifies security management and enables advanced threat protection across hybrid cloud workloads.

- **Benefit:** Offers increased visibility and control over the security of your cloud resources.

Azure DDoS Protection:

- **Solution:** Provides enhanced DDoS mitigation features to protect Azure applications.

- **Benefit:** Defends against DDoS attacks, maintaining availability and performance.

5. Case Studies: SMEs and Cloud Security Success Stories

Case Study 1: Retail SME Implements Strong Access Control

- **Background:** A small online retailer chose to implement MFA across its cloud services.

- **Action:** MFA was deployed to add an extra layer of security for accessing cloud-stored customer data.

- **Result:** The retailer saw a significant decrease in unauthorised access attempts.

Case Study 2: Healthcare SME Focuses on Compliance

- **Situation:** A healthcare provider needed to ensure compliance with HIPAA for its cloud-stored patient records.

- **Measures:** Adopted encrypted storage solutions and conducted regular compliance audits.

- **Impact:** Successfully passed audits and increased patient trust due to enhanced data protection measures.

Conclusion

Small and medium-sized enterprises (SMEs) need to ensure that their cloud security is up to par. However, this can be a challenging task. By implementing the best practices mentioned above and consistently assessing and refining their security strategies, SMEs can protect their digital assets. Effective cloud security measures are important to safeguard sensitive information, ensure compliance, and ultimately, build trust with customers. This is especially important for small to medium-sized businesses that operate in the digital age.

CHAPTER 10: REGULATORY COMPLIANCE AND CYBER LAW

As digital landscapes evolve, so too do the complexities of cybersecurity laws and regulations designed to protect sensitive data and maintain privacy. This detailed overview will explore the latest developments in global cybersecurity legislation, focusing on the strategic responses and regulatory frameworks that are shaping cybersecurity protocols around the worlds

1. Understanding Cyber Law and Regulatory Compliance

Cyber law refers to the legal principles and legislation that govern the use of the internet and digital technologies. It encompasses issues related to digital communication, privacy, data protection, and cybersecurity measures.

Regulatory compliance in cybersecurity involves adhering to laws and regulations established by governmental bodies to protect data and prevent breaches. Non-compliance can result in legal penalties, financial losses, and damage to an organization's reputation.

2. Key Global Cybersecurity Laws and Regulations

United States:

In the U.S., a range of federal and state laws govern cybersecurity.

- The Health Insurance Portability and Accountability Act (**HIPAA**) mandates protections for patient health information,

- while the Gramm-Leach-Bliley Act (**GLBA**) oversees the safeguarding of financial information.

- The Payment Card Industry Data Security Standard (**PCI DSS**) sets requirements for entities handling credit card data.

- Recent developments include the expansion of the New York Department of Financial Services (**NYDFS**) cybersecurity regulation, which now demands more stringent notification procedures in the wake of a ransomware deployment.

European Union:

The EU continues to strengthen its cybersecurity framework.

- The General Data Protection Regulation (**GDPR**) remains a cornerstone, setting rigorous standards for data privacy and security.

- The Network and Information Systems (**NIS**) Directive, recently updated to NIS 2.0, aims to improve the resilience of network and information systems across the EU.

This directive now includes stringent reporting requirements for sectors deemed essential, including energy, transportation, and health).

United Kingdom:

The UK's approach to cybersecurity is outlined in the Data Protection Act (**DPA**) 2018, which aligns closely with the **GDPR**, focusing on the secure processing of personal data. Additionally, the Network and Information Systems (NIS) Regulations have been updated to protect essential services from cyber threats.

3. Compliance Strategies

To effectively comply with various cyber laws and regulations, organizations can adopt several strategic approaches:

Risk Assessment and Management

- **Conduct Regular Assessments:** Regularly evaluate your data handling and processing activities to identify risks and vulnerabilities.

- **Implement Risk Management Processes:** Develop and implement processes to mitigate identified risks, ensuring that protective measures and responses are in place.

Data Protection Measures

- **Encrypt Sensitive Data:** Use strong encryption to protect data in transit and at rest.

- **Secure Access Controls:** Limit access to sensitive data to only those who need it to perform their job functions.

Training and Awareness Programs

- **Regular Training:** Conduct training sessions for employees on the importance of data protection and the specific compliance requirements of the organization.

- **Update Policies:** Regularly update training materials and policies to reflect new regulatory developments and compliance requirements.

Audit and Monitoring

- **Regular Audits:** Perform regular audits to ensure compliance with both internal policies and external regulatory requirements.

- **Continuous Monitoring:** Use tools and systems to monitor the handling and protection of sensitive data continuously.

4. Challenges in Implementing Cybersecurity Laws

One of the biggest challenges is keeping up with the rapid pace of technological changes and the evolving tactics of cybercriminals. Laws must be continually revised to close any security gaps that might emerge. Additionally, ensuring that these laws are enforced consistently across different sectors and regions adds another layer of complexity.

Why Compliance Matters

Failing to comply with these laws can lead to hefty fines and damage to an organisation's reputation. It's not just about avoiding penalties; effective compliance helps protect customer data and enhances trust in a company's brand.

Looking Ahead: Future Trends in Cybersecurity Legislation

As digital technologies advance, we can expect cybersecurity laws to become more rigorous and detailed. Future regulations will likely address emerging technologies like artificial intelligence and the increasing use of the Internet of Things (IoT), which are becoming integral to business operations and everyday life.

Businesses must stay proactive, not only to meet current legal requirements but also to prepare for future changes. This means regularly updating security measures, conducting thorough risk assessments, and maintaining a clear understanding of both global and local cybersecurity regulations.

Conclusion

Understanding and complying with cyber law and regulatory requirements is crucial for organizations operating in the digital space. By implementing comprehensive compliance strategies, organizations can protect themselves from legal penalties and build trust with customers and partners by demonstrating a commitment to data security and privacy. Regular updates to compliance strategies are necessary to keep pace with evolving regulations and cyber threats.

THE IMPLICATIONS OF GDPR, HIPAA, AND OTHER REGULATIONS ON GLOBAL OPERATIONS

In today's globalized economy, businesses often operate across multiple jurisdictions, encountering a variety of legal landscapes when it comes to data protection and privacy laws. Key regulations such as the General Data Protection Regulation (GDPR) in the European Union and the Health Insurance Portability and Accountability Act (HIPAA) in the United States have significant implications for how organizations handle personal and sensitive information. Understanding these implications is crucial for maintaining compliance and ensuring the secure handling of data across borders.

1. General Data Protection Regulation (GDPR)

The GDPR is one of the most influential and comprehensive data protection laws globally. It came into effect on May 25, 2018, and impacts any organization operating within the EU, as well as organizations outside of the EU that offer goods or services to customers or businesses in the EU.

Key Requirements of GDPR:

Consent: Organizations must obtain clear and explicit consent from individuals before collecting their data.

- **Right to Access:** Individuals have the right to access their data and information about how this data is being processed.

- **Data Portability:** Individuals have the right to receive their data and transfer it to another controller.

- **Breach Notification:** In the event of a data breach, organizations must notify the appropriate data protection authority within 72 hours, where feasible.

- **Right to be Forgotten:** Individuals can demand the deletion of their data when it's no longer necessary for the purpose it was collected, among other conditions.

Implications for Global Operations:

Operational Changes: Organizations must ensure that their data handling and processing activities are transparent and comply with GDPR. This may require significant changes in how data is collected, stored, and used.

- **Increased Costs:** Compliance can increase operational costs, including investment in security technologies, staff training, and potentially, hiring data protection officers.

- **Legal Accountability:** Non-compliance can lead to heavy fines, up to 4% of annual global turnover or €20 million, whichever is greater.

2. Health Insurance Portability and Accountability Act (HIPAA)

HIPAA is a U.S. regulation that protects the privacy and security of certain health information. Established in 1996, it sets standards for the protection of health information held by covered entities and their business associates.

Key Components of HIPAA:

- **Privacy Rule:** Protects the privacy of individually identifiable health information.

- **Security Rule:** Sets standards for the security of electronically protected health information.

- **Breach Notification Rule:** Requires covered entities to notify affected individuals, the U.S. Department of Health & Human Services, and in some cases, the media of a breach of unsecured protected health information.

Implications for Global Operations:

- **Compliance Requirements:** Any organization dealing with **protected health information** (PHI) must ensure that they have adequate security measures in place to protect data and comply with HIPAA.

- **Business Associate Agreements (BAAs):** U.S.-based companies, or any global company handling U.S. health data, must ensure that their partners and vendors sign BAAs that obligate them to protect PHI as outlined by HIPAA.

- **Financial Risks:** Violations of HIPAA can lead to significant financial penalties, which can impact the financial status of an organization.

3. Gramm-Leach-Bliley Act (GLBA)

The Gramm-Leach-Bliley Act (GLBA), also known as the Financial Services Modernization Act of 1999, is a crucial law in the United States that helps protect personal financial information held by financial institutions and other companies that offer financial services or products, like loans, financial advice, or insurance.

What is the Gramm-Leach-Bliley Act?

The GLBA sets out to ensure that financial institutions are transparent about how they handle consumer information and mandates that they must protect data diligently. Here's a simple breakdown of what GLBA involves:

Privacy Notices:

Financial institutions must provide clear explanations to their customers about what personal information they collect, how they use it, and how they protect it. Customers should also be informed about their rights to opt out of some forms of data sharing.

Data Security:

Institutions are required to put strong security measures in place to protect sensitive data from threats and breaches. This involves creating detailed security plans that outline how they will safeguard customer information.

Limits on Data Sharing:

The act restricts how financial institutions can share sensitive personal financial information with non-affiliated third parties. Customers have the right to opt out of some forms of information sharing, giving them more control over their data.

Why is GLBA Important?

For consumers, GLBA assures that financial institutions are handling their personal information with care and responsibility. It gives consumers certain rights over their personal information and ensures they are informed about privacy practices.

For businesses, GLBA compliance is critical—not only to avoid hefty fines but also to maintain trust and integrity. Ensuring compliance helps protect against data breaches and unauthorized use of consumer data, which can have severe reputational and financial consequences for businesses.

4. Payment Card Industry Data Security Standard (PCI DSS)

The Payment Card Industry Data Security Standard (PCI DSS) is a set of requirements designed to ensure that all companies that accept, process, store, or transmit credit card information maintain a secure environment. Essentially, PCI DSS aims to protect cardholder data from fraud and theft, safeguarding both the interests of consumers and the integrity of the financial system.

Understanding PCI DSS: Simple Explanation

What is PCI DSS?

PCI DSS stands for Payment Card Industry Data Security Standard. It was developed by the major credit card companies as a guideline to help prevent credit card fraud, hacking, and various other security vulnerabilities and threats.

Who needs to comply?

Any organization, regardless of size or number of transactions, that accepts, transmits, or stores any cardholder data must comply with PCI DSS.

Key Requirements of PCI DSS

PCI DSS has several requirements which are aimed at creating a secure network and protecting cardholder data:

Build and Maintain a Secure Network:

- Install and maintain a firewall configuration to protect cardholder data.

- Do not use vendor-supplied defaults for system passwords and other security parameters.

Protect Cardholder Data:

- Protect stored cardholder data.

- Encrypt transmission of cardholder data across open, public networks.

Maintain a Vulnerability Management Program:

- Use and regularly update anti-virus software or programs.

- Develop and maintain secure systems and applications.

Implement Strong Access Control Measures:

- Restrict access to cardholder data by business need-to-know.

- Assign a unique ID to each person with computer access.

- Restrict physical access to cardholder data.

Regularly Monitor and Test Networks:

- Track and monitor all access to network resources and cardholder data.

- Regularly test security systems and processes.

Maintain an Information Security Policy:

- Maintain a policy that addresses information security for employees and contractors.

Importance of PCI DSS Compliance

Complying with PCI DSS is not just about avoiding penalties but about protecting sensitive cardholder data from breaches and thefts, which can lead to significant financial losses and damage to a company's reputation. It's crucial for maintaining trust between merchants and their customers.

Challenges and Best Practices

- **Implementation Challenges:** Small businesses might find the cost and complexity of implementing all the PCI DSS requirements challenging.

- **Best Practices:** Start with a risk assessment to prioritize actions, focus on the most critical vulnerabilities first, and consider using professional services if needed to ensure compliance.

By adhering to PCI DSS, businesses can ensure that their payment card operations are secure and that they are doing their part to protect consumers against the risks associated with card payment environments.

5. New York Department of Financial Services (NYDFS)

The New York Department of Financial Services (NYDFS) cybersecurity regulation is a set of standards aimed at enhancing the cybersecurity of financial institutions. This regulation, known officially as 23 NYCRR 500, is significant because it was one of the first of its kind in the United States to mandate specific cybersecurity practices for financial services companies.

Overview of NYDFS Cybersecurity Regulation

Who is affected?

The regulation applies to all financial services institutions that operate under a license, registration, or charter authorised by the NYDFS. This includes banks, insurance companies, and other financial services providers.

Key Requirements:

- **Cybersecurity Program:** Each company must maintain a cybersecurity program designed to protect the confidentiality, integrity, and availability of its information systems.

- **Cybersecurity Policy:** Companies are required to implement a written policy or policies, approved by senior management, setting out the company's practices and procedures to protect its information systems and nonpublic information.

- **Chief Information Security Officer:** Companies need to designate a qualified individual who will oversee and implement the cybersecurity program and enforce its policy.

- **Penetration Testing and Vulnerability Assessments:** Regular testing and assessments are mandatory to ensure that the systems are secure and any vulnerabilities are addressed.

- **Audit Trail:** Companies must maintain systems that can reconstruct material financial transactions to support normal operations in the event of a cybersecurity incident.

- **Access Privileges:** Companies must limit user access privileges to information systems that provide access to nonpublic information.

- **Third-Party Service Providers:** Companies must have policies and procedures in place to ensure the security of information systems and nonpublic information that are accessible to, or held by, third-party service providers.

Incident Reporting:

Companies must report any cybersecurity events to the NYDFS as soon as possible but no later than 72 hours after becoming aware of the event.

Importance of NYDFS Cybersecurity Regulation

The NYDFS cybersecurity regulation is crucial because it sets a high standard for cybersecurity practices within the financial sector. It aims to protect financial data and systems from unauthorised access, use, or other malicious acts that could harm the public. Compliance is not just about following the law but protecting customers and maintaining their trust by safeguarding their personal and financial information.

Challenges and Best Practices for Compliance

Challenges:

- Implementing comprehensive cybersecurity programs can be complex and costly, especially for smaller institutions.

- Keeping up with evolving compliance requirements and cybersecurity threats requires continuous effort and investment.

Best Practices:

- Regular training and education programs for employees to ensure they understand their roles in maintaining cybersecurity.

- Employing strong encryption methods for storing and transmitting data.

- Engaging in regular audits and assessments to identify and address vulnerabilities.

- By complying with the NYDFS cybersecurity regulation, financial institutions not only adhere to legal requirements but also build robust defences against cyber threats, thereby protecting their customers' sensitive data and maintaining the integrity of the financial system.

6. Global Compliance Strategies

- **Adaptation to Local Laws:** Businesses must adapt their operations to meet the requirements of local laws wherever they operate, ensuring compliance with not just GDPR and HIPAA, but other local data protection laws.

- **Unified Data Protection Strategy:** Implementing a comprehensive data protection strategy that can accommodate the most stringent regulations is a prudent approach to ensure compliance across different regions.

- **Regular Training and Audits:** Regular training programs for employees and periodic audits of data protection practices help maintain compliance and safeguard against data breaches.

Conclusion

Regulations like GDPR and HIPAA exemplify the growing importance of data protection and privacy laws worldwide. As businesses expand globally, understanding and integrating these regulations into their operations is crucial. Failure to comply can result in severe penalties, loss of trust, and financial harm. Conversely, robust compliance can enhance a company's reputation, build consumer trust, and provide a competitive advantage in the global marketplace.

CHAPTER 11: INCIDENT RESPONSE AND DISASTER RECOVERY

In the realm of cybersecurity, having robust incident response and disaster recovery plans is crucial. These plans ensure that an organisation can quickly manage and mitigate the effects of a cyberattack or any unexpected disaster that impacts data integrity and availability. This guide explains the fundamentals of incident response and disaster recovery, detailing how to plan and execute effective strategies to protect organisational assets.

1. Understanding Incident Response and Disaster Recovery

Incident Response (IR) is a set of procedures an organization follows in response to a cyberattack or data breach. The goal is to handle the situation in a way that limits damage and reduces recovery time and costs.

Disaster Recovery (DR) is part of a broader approach that includes restoring data and systems to their normal status after a disaster. It's focused on the continuity of operations and the minimization of business downtime.

2. Key Phases of Incident Response

Effective incident response strategies are typically structured in phases. Here's a breakdown of each phase:

Preparation

- **Training and Awareness:** Regularly train staff on their roles during an incident. Ensure that everyone knows what actions to take when a breach occurs.

- **Tools and Resources:** Equip your team with the necessary tools and resources to detect, analyze, and mitigate breaches. This includes software for monitoring systems and communications tools for effective coordination.

Identification

- **Detection Tools:** Utilize advanced detection tools to identify anomalies that suggest a security incident.

- **Alert System:** Set up an alert system that promptly notifies the incident response team when potential threats are detected.

Containment

- **Short-term Containment:** This immediate response aims to limit the spread of the incident. For example, if a particular system is compromised, disconnecting it from the network might be necessary.

- **Long-term Containment:** Involves implementing changes to prevent a recurrence. This might include strengthening firewall rules or updating access controls.

Eradication

- **Remove Threats:** Once containment is secured, identify and remove the root causes of the incident. This might involve deleting malicious files and disabling breached user accounts.

- **System Cleanup:** Ensure that any malware is completely removed from systems before they are restored to normal operations.

Recovery

- **System Restoration:** Begin to restore and return affected systems and devices to their operational state.

- **Monitoring:** Closely monitor the systems for any signs of issues to ensure that all aspects of the threat have been eradicated.

Lessons Learned

- **Review and Analysis:** After managing the incident, conduct a thorough review of how it was handled and document any lessons learned.

- **Update Response Strategies:** Use the insights gained to improve the incident response plan. This might involve training, changes in policy, or additional tools.

3. Disaster Recovery Planning

A **disaster recovery plan (DRP)** is crucial for maintaining continuity and quick recovery. Key elements include:

Backup Solutions

Regular Backups: Ensure regular backups of all critical information to secure offsite locations. Test recovery from these backups to ensure they work.

Recovery Strategies

- **Define Critical Systems:** Identify which systems and data are critical for the business's operation and focus on their recovery.

- **Recovery Objectives:** Establish Recovery Time Objectives (RTO) and Recovery Point Objectives (RPO) for different business processes.

Communication Plan

- **Internal Communication:** Detail how to communicate within the team and to the entire organization during a disaster.

- **External Communication:** Prepare templates for communicating with external stakeholders, including customers, regulators, and the media.

4. Execution and Maintenance

- **Regular Drills:** Conduct regular drills to ensure that everyone knows their roles during an actual incident or disaster.

- **Plan Updates:** Regularly review and update the DRP and IR plan to adapt to new threats, technological changes, or structural changes within the organization.

Conclusion

Effective incident response and disaster recovery planning are about preparedness and resilience. By understanding these processes and meticulously planning, organizations can withstand cyberattacks and other disasters with minimal damage and swift recovery. The key is continuous improvement and adaptation to the evolving landscape of threats.

DISASTER RECOVERY PLANS (DRPS)

In today's digitally driven world, businesses rely heavily on data and IT systems. Disruptions, whether from natural disasters, cyberattacks, or technological failures, can lead to significant downtime and data loss, impacting business operations severely. This chapter focuses on how to create and manage effective disaster recovery plans (DRPs) to minimize downtime and data loss, ensuring businesses can quickly resume operations after a disruption.

1. Understanding the Importance of Disaster Recovery Planning

Disaster recovery planning is a crucial part of business continuity strategies. It involves preparing for and recovering from events that can disrupt normal business operations. The goal is to maintain or quickly resume mission-critical functions following a disaster.

Key Benefits of Disaster Recovery Planning Include:

- Reducing potential economic loss.

- Decreasing the likelihood of downtime.

- Minimizing data loss.

- Protecting the organization's reputation.

- Ensuring compliance with industry regulations.

2. Elements of a Disaster Recovery Plan

A comprehensive disaster recovery plan should address several key components to ensure it is effective and actionable.

Risk Assessment and Business Impact Analysis (BIA):

- **Risk Assessment:** Identify potential threats to business operations, including natural disasters, cyber threats, hardware failures, and power outages.

- **Business Impact Analysis:** Assess the potential impacts of these disruptions on business operations. Determine which systems and processes are critical for the business's survival and understand the maximum tolerable downtime for each.

- **Recovery Strategies:**

     Develop strategies for data backup, system recovery, and alternative work arrangements. Choose appropriate technologies and processes to restore hardware, applications, and data in time to meet the needs of the business recovery.

Plan Development:

- **Document the Plan:** Write down the plan, including recovery protocols and procedures. Define roles and responsibilities clearly.

- **Communication Plan:** Establish a communication strategy to notify and instruct employees during and after a disaster. Include contact information for key personnel and external contacts like suppliers and emergency responders.

3. Basic Incident Response Plan Template

Creating an effective incident response plan (IRP) and having a robust disaster recovery strategy are critical components of any organisation's cybersecurity posture.

1. Preparation

- **Team and Roles:** List key response team members and define their roles and responsibilities. Include contact information.

- **Tools and Resources:** Identify and prepare the tools, technologies, and physical resources needed to detect and respond to incidents.

2. Identification

- **Detection Methods:** Define how incidents are identified (e.g., monitoring tools, and employee reports).

- **Incident Logging:** Specify how incidents should be logged and reported, including the details that need to be collected.

3. Containment

- **Short-term:** Outline immediate steps to limit the impact of an incident, such as isolating the affected system.

- **Long-term:** Plan for additional measures if the incident is larger or more complex than initially thought.

4. Eradication

- **Removal of Threats:** Describe the processes to eliminate the root cause of the incident and any associated threats or vulnerabilities.

- **Validation:** Ensure that the systems are clean and that no threats remain.

5. Recovery

- **System Restoration:** Define steps to bring affected systems back to operational status.

- **Testing and Monitoring:** Plan for testing systems to ensure they are functioning as expected and monitor for any signs of weakness that could be exploited again.

6. Lessons Learned

- **Review and Analysis:** After an incident, hold a debriefing meeting to discuss what happened, how it was handled, and what could be improved.

- **Update Plan:** Regularly update the incident response plan based on lessons learned and new potential threats.

4. Implementing the Disaster Recovery Plan

Infrastructure and Technology:

Invest in the right technology to support backup and recovery processes. This might include cloud storage solutions for data redundancy, backup generators for power failures, and secure remote access solutions for staff.

Testing and Maintenance:

- Regularly test the DRP to ensure its effectiveness. Simulate different types of disasters to uncover any weaknesses in the plan.

- Update the plan regularly to accommodate new business processes, technological changes, and evolving threats.

Training and Awareness:

- Train staff on their specific roles and responsibilities as outlined in the DRP. Ensure everyone understands the steps they need to take during a disaster.

- Foster a culture of resilience and preparedness within the organization by regularly discussing the importance of disaster recovery and continuous improvements to the plan.

5. Monitoring and Evaluating the Disaster Recovery Plan

Continuous Improvement:

- Monitor the effectiveness of the DRP continuously. Use lessons learned from tests and actual incidents to refine and improve the plan.

- Stay informed about new technologies and best practices that can enhance the disaster recovery process.

Feedback Mechanism:

- Encourage feedback from employees on the disaster recovery process. Employee insights can be valuable in identifying potential improvements.

- Regularly review and revise the DRP to reflect new insights and feedback.

6. Real-world case Studies

Discuss several case studies where effective disaster recovery planning minimised downtime and data loss. Analyse both successful implementations and instances where recovery did not go as planned. Lessons learned from these real-world examples can provide valuable insights into best practices and common pitfalls.

7. Best Practices for Disaster Recovery Planning

1. Risk Assessment

Conduct a thorough risk assessment to identify critical systems and data that need protection. Understanding what the most valuable assets are will help prioritise recovery efforts.

2. Backup Solutions

Implement regular backup procedures for all critical data. Ensure backups are stored in a secure, off-site location. Test backups regularly to confirm data can be recovered effectively.

3. Recovery Objectives

Define clear recovery time objectives (RTO) and recovery point objectives (RPO). These metrics will guide the recovery process and set expectations for how quickly systems need to be restored after a disruption.

4. Communication Plan

Develop a communication plan that outlines how to notify employees, customers, and stakeholders in the event of a disaster. Keeping everyone informed is crucial for managing a crisis effectively.

5. Training and Testing

Regular training on disaster recovery procedures is essential for preparing your team to act quickly and effectively. Conduct drills and simulations to test your disaster recovery plan and make improvements based on the outcomes.

Conclusion

In conclusion, creating and managing an effective disaster recovery plan is essential for minimizing downtime and data loss. By understanding critical operations, implementing robust recovery strategies, regularly testing and updating the plan, and fostering a culture of preparedness, businesses can enhance their resilience against disasters. This proactive approach not only safeguards data and systems but also supports overall business continuity and stability.

CHAPTER 12: ADVANCED THREAT PROTECTION AND VULNERABILITY MANAGEMENT

In the complex and ever-evolving world of cybersecurity, advanced threat protection and effective vulnerability management are critical components of a robust security strategy. This chapter aims to educate readers on sophisticated methodologies for threat protection and response and to provide insight into best practices for vulnerability assessment and management. Through detailed explanations and strategic recommendations, this chapter serves as a comprehensive guide for enhancing organizational security postures.

1. Advanced Threat Protection Strategies

Advanced threat protection (ATP) involves deploying cutting-edge technologies and methodologies to detect, prevent, and respond to new and evolving cyber threats. This section will outline the key strategies that constitute an advanced approach to threat protection.

A. Machine Learning and Artificial Intelligence in Threat Detection

- **Description:** Utilize AI and machine learning algorithms to analyze patterns and predict potential threats based on data from past incidents.

- **Application:** Implement systems that dynamically learn from continuous data input to identify anomalies that may indicate a cybersecurity threat, such as unusual access patterns or unexpected information flows.

B. Behavior-Based Detection

- **Description:** Go beyond signature-based detection methods to analyze the behaviour of applications and network traffic.

- **Application:** Deploy systems that monitor for behaviours indicative of malicious activity, such as rapid data encryption that may signify a ransomware attack.

C. Threat Intelligence Platforms

- **Description:** Use comprehensive threat intelligence gathered from various sources to inform security measures.

- **Application:** Integrate real-time threat data from global sources into security systems to enhance the detection of threats and enable proactive defence measures.

2. Response Mechanisms and Incident Management

Effective incident response is crucial for minimizing the impact of security breaches. This section discusses advanced methodologies in crafting a response to detected threats.

A. Automated Response and Remediation

- **Description:** Implement automation in the response to security threats to speed up containment and remediation processes.

- **Application:** Use automated scripts or tools to isolate infected systems, apply security patches, or block malicious IP addresses automatically upon detection of a threat.

B. Orchestration of Response Activities

- **Description:** Coordinate various security tools and processes for a unified response strategy.

- **Application:** Employ orchestration platforms to synchronize actions across different security solutions, such as firewall rules, intrusion prevention systems, and endpoint protection, ensuring a cohesive and effective response to incidents.

C. Post-Incident Analysis and Forensics

- **Description:** Conduct detailed investigations following an incident to determine the cause and extract lessons learned.

- **Application:** Use forensic tools to analyze compromised systems, trace back the origins of an attack, and understand how the breach occurred to prevent future incidents.

3. Vulnerability Assessment and Management Best Practices

Vulnerability management is a proactive approach to discovering, assessing, and mitigating security vulnerabilities within an organization's network.

A. Continuous Vulnerability Scanning

- **Description:** Regularly scan systems and networks to identify vulnerabilities that could be exploited by attackers.

- **Application:** Implement automated scanning tools that continuously monitor the network for vulnerabilities, providing alerts when potential risks are identified.

B. Prioritization of Risks

- **Description:** Prioritize vulnerabilities based on their potential impact and the likelihood of exploitation.

- **Application:** Use a risk-based approach to focus remediation efforts on the most critical vulnerabilities first, such as those that affect sensitive data or critical infrastructure.

C. Patch Management

- Description: Ensure timely application of patches to fix vulnerabilities in software and systems.

- Application: Develop a systematic patch management policy that includes routine checks for software updates and the prompt deployment of patches to vulnerable systems.

D. Regular Security Audits

- **Description:** Conduct comprehensive audits to assess the effectiveness of existing security measures.

- **Application:** Schedule periodic security audits conducted by internal teams or external experts to review security policies, control effectiveness, and compliance with regulatory standards.

6. Continual Improvement

The threat landscape and organisational needs are always evolving. Regularly review and update your disaster recovery plan to accommodate new technologies, processes, and potential threats.

Implementing these strategies will help ensure that your organisation is prepared to respond effectively to security incidents and recover swiftly from disruptions, minimising impact and downtime. Remember, the key to successful incident response and disaster recovery is preparation, regular testing, and continuous improvement.

Conclusion

Advancing threat protection and enhancing vulnerability management are imperative for safeguarding an organisation's digital assets against increasingly sophisticated cyber threats. By employing the methodologies and best practices outlined in this chapter, organisations can develop a resilient security posture that not only reacts effectively to incidents but also prevents potential breaches through proactive measures. This holistic approach to cybersecurity ensures the integrity, confidentiality, and availability of information in a challenging digital landscape.

INTRUSION DETECTION SYSTEMS (IDS) AND INTRUSION PREVENTION SYSTEMS (IPS)

In the realm of cybersecurity, advanced security solutions such as Intrusion Detection Systems (IDS) and Intrusion Prevention Systems (IPS) are critical tools in the arsenal against cyber threats. These systems help organizations detect and prevent unauthorized access or attacks on their networks. Understanding how IDS and IPS work and how they can be effectively utilized is essential for maintaining robust network security.

What are IDS and IPS?

Intrusion Detection Systems (IDS) are designed to monitor network traffic and identify suspicious activities that could indicate a security breach. When an IDS detects a potential threat, it sends an alert to the system administrator. Essentially, IDS acts as a surveillance system, monitoring for signs of potential threats based on predefined rules or suspicious patterns.

Intrusion Prevention Systems (IPS), on the other hand, not only detect potential threats but also take immediate action to prevent the threat from causing harm. IPS can block malicious traffic, prevent the exploitation of vulnerabilities, and even stop the spread of an attack within a network. IPS can be thought of as the next step beyond IDS, providing not just alerts but also proactive protection.

How Do IDS and IPS Work?

Traffic Monitoring:

Both IDS and IPS continuously monitor network traffic to identify unusual behaviour or patterns that might indicate malicious activity. This monitoring can be based on signatures of known threats or anomalies that deviate from normal network behaviour.

Alert System:

In the case of IDS, once a threat is detected, the system alerts the network administrator or a security analyst who then decides how to respond. IDS does not take direct action to block the threat.IPS, meanwhile, is configured to automatically take action against detected threats without waiting for human intervention, effectively stopping attacks in real time.

Threat Prevention:

IPS can block access or quarantine a suspicious file based on its threat analysis, thereby preventing damage before it starts. This is particularly useful for stopping the spread of malware or shutting down attempts to exploit vulnerabilities.

Best Practices for Using IDS and IPS

1. Proper Configuration and Updates:

- Ensure that both IDS and IPS are properly configured to match the security needs of your organization. This includes setting appropriate rules and signatures to detect and respond to threats effectively.

- Regular updates are crucial, as cyber threats constantly evolve. Keeping the systems updated ensures they can recognize and defend against the latest threats.

2. Integration with Other Security Measures:

- IDS and IPS should not be used in isolation. Integrating these systems with other security measures such as firewalls, anti-malware software, and encryption tools provides a layered defence strategy, enhancing overall network security.

3. Regular Audits and Reviews:

- Conduct regular security audits to ensure IDS and IPS are performing as expected. This includes reviewing alert logs, adjusting configurations, and updating rules based on new vulnerabilities.

4. Training and Awareness:

- Train staff to understand the alerts generated by IDS and how to respond appropriately. For IPS, ensure that staff understand how and why certain actions are taken automatically to prevent false alarms from disrupting legitimate activities.

Conclusion

IDS and IPS are sophisticated tools that, when effectively utilised, provide a crucial layer of security for detecting and preventing cyber threats. Their proactive monitoring and preventive actions enable organisations to respond to threats swiftly, minimising potential damage. By integrating IDS and IPS into a comprehensive cybersecurity strategy and maintaining their operations through regular updates and reviews, organisations can significantly enhance their defensive posture against various cyber threats.

CHAPTER 13: CYBERSECURITY IN EMERGING TECHNOLOGIES

As technology continues to evolve at a rapid pace, new advancements such as blockchain, the Internet of Things (IoT), and other emerging technologies are reshaping industries and introducing unique security challenges. This chapter aims to provide a thorough exploration of the cybersecurity considerations specific to these technologies. It will also discuss strategies to secure future technological innovations, ensuring that organizations can embrace new technologies while minimizing their cybersecurity risks.

1. Understanding Emerging Technologies and Their Cybersecurity Implications

This section will introduce each technology, explain how it works, and discuss the specific cybersecurity risks associated with it.

A. Blockchain Technology

- **Description:** Blockchain is a distributed ledger technology known for its key features: decentralization, immutability, and transparency. It underpins cryptocurrencies like Bitcoin and has applications in various sectors including finance, healthcare, and supply chain management.

- **Security Considerations:** While blockchain is praised for its security due to cryptographic hashing and decentralized nature, it is not impervious to attacks. Issues such as the 51% attack, smart contract vulnerabilities, and code exploitation in decentralized applications can pose significant risks.

B. Internet of Things (IoT)

- **Description:** IoT involves extending internet connectivity to everyday objects, enabling them to send and receive data. This interconnectedness offers immense convenience and efficiency but also increases the attack surfaces for cyber threats.

- **Security Considerations:** IoT devices often lack robust built-in security, making them vulnerable to hacking. Common risks include unauthorized access, data theft, and turning these devices into nodes in botnet attacks.

C. Other Emerging Technologies

- **Description:** Technologies like artificial intelligence (AI), machine learning (ML), and 5G also bring new dimensions to cybersecurity.

- **Security Considerations:** AI and ML systems can be manipulated through data poisoning or adversarial attacks, while 5G's vast connectivity potential can expand vulnerabilities, particularly in the areas of user privacy and mobile network security.

2. Securing Future Technological Innovations

This section will explore forward-looking strategies to ensure the security of technologies still in the developmental or conceptual stages.

A. Proactive Threat Intelligence

- **Strategy:** Leverage threat intelligence to predict and prepare for potential cyber threats before they materialize.

- **Application:** Stay abreast of new malware types and hacking techniques that could target next-generation technologies.

B. Collaborative Security Frameworks

- **Strategy:** Foster collaboration across industry players to develop and share robust security frameworks and best practices.

- **Application:** Participate in consortiums and working groups that focus on creating standardized security protocols for new technologies.

C. Ethical Hacking and Penetration Testing

- **Strategy:** Employ ethical hackers to identify and resolve security vulnerabilities within new technologies.

- **Application:** Regularly schedule penetration testing for emerging technology systems to identify vulnerabilities that could be exploited by malicious actors.

Conclusion

Adopting emerging technologies comes with transformative potential but also significant cybersecurity risks. By understanding these risks and implementing strategic measures, organizations can protect themselves against cyber threats while harnessing the benefits of innovation.

SECURITY IMPLICATIONS OF EMERGING TECHNOLOGIES SUCH AS IOT, 5G, AND SMART CITIES

Emerging technologies such as the Internet of Things (IoT), 5G networks, and smart cities are transforming how we interact with our surroundings and manage resources, leading to more efficient, automated, and connected societies. However, these advancements also introduce significant security challenges that must be addressed to protect individuals, businesses, and the infrastructure itself. Let's explore the security implications of these technologies and offer some guidelines for securing devices and networks in these new environments.

Security Implications of Emerging Technologies

1. Internet of Things (IoT):

IoT devices, ranging from smart home appliances to health monitors, are increasingly common in our daily lives. These devices often collect and transmit sensitive data, making them targets for cyber attacks.

- **Vulnerabilities:** Many IoT devices have weak security settings by default, use insecure network services, and often receive infrequent updates, making them easy targets for hackers.

- **Data Privacy:** The vast amount of data collected by IoT devices can include personal information, creating privacy concerns and increasing the risk of data breaches.

2. 5G Networks:

5G technology promises faster speeds and more reliable internet connections, but it also raises significant security concerns.

- **Expanded Attack Surface:** The increased number of connected devices and services supported by 5G networks enlarges the potential attack surface for cybercriminals.

- **Network Security:** The decentralized nature of 5G technology, which relies more on software than hardware, introduces new vulnerabilities that can be exploited by attackers.

3. Smart Cities:

Smart cities use IoT and other technologies to improve the efficiency of services such as transportation, energy, and emergency services. While beneficial, this interconnectedness poses significant security risks.

- **Systemic Risks:** A cyber attack on one part of a smart city's infrastructure could potentially have wide-reaching effects, impacting everything from traffic systems to water supply.

- **Complexity of Systems:** The integration of various technologies and the sheer scale of data processing make it difficult to secure smart city infrastructures comprehensively.

Guidelines for Securing Devices and Networks

For IoT Devices:

- **Change Default Settings:** Always change default passwords and settings on new IoT devices to strong, unique alternatives.

- **Regular Updates:** Ensure your devices are regularly updated with the latest firmware and software patches to protect against known vulnerabilities.

- **Secure Network Practices:** Connect IoT devices to a secure network, ideally separate from the main business or home network to contain potential breaches.

For 5G Networks:

- **Enhanced Encryption:** Utilize strong encryption protocols for data transmitted over 5G networks to protect against eavesdropping and data theft.

- **Network Segmentation:** Segment networks limit an attacker's ability to move laterally across the network once access is gained.

- **Regular Security Assessments:** Continuously monitor and assess the security posture of your 5G networks to detect and respond to threats promptly.

For Smart Cities:

Integrated Security Solutions: Develop a unified security strategy that covers all aspects of the smart city's infrastructure.

- **Public-Private Partnerships:** Collaborate with technology providers, security experts, and other stakeholders to enhance security measures and share best practices.

- **Incident Response Plans:** Prepare comprehensive incident response plans to quickly address and mitigate the effects of a cyber attack on critical infrastructure.

Conclusion

By understanding the risks associated with IoT, 5G, and smart cities and implementing robust security measures, we can harness the benefits of these technologies while minimizing their potential threats. The key is proactive security management and ongoing vigilance to adapt to the evolving cyber landscape.

CHAPTER 14: STRATEGIC CYBERSECURITY LEADERSHIP(CTO)

In the digital age, strategic leadership in cybersecurity is paramount for any organisation aiming to protect its assets from cyber threats. This chapter delves into the critical role of Chief Technology Officers (CTOs) in leading strategic cybersecurity initiatives and outlines best practices for building and leading effective cross-functional cybersecurity teams. By exploring these areas, the chapter aims to equip CTOs and other leaders with the knowledge and strategies needed to enhance their organization's cybersecurity posture.

1. The Role of CTOs in Cybersecurity

This section will focus on the pivotal role of CTOs in shaping and steering the cybersecurity strategies within an organization.

A. Defining the Role and Responsibilities

- **Overview:** The CTO typically oversees the development and implementation of technology within an organization, ensuring that IT infrastructure and applications are secure against potential threats.

- **Cybersecurity Focus:** As part of their role, CTOs must have a comprehensive understanding of the current cybersecurity landscape, including emerging threats and innovative defence mechanisms.

B. Strategic Planning and Policy Development

- **Strategy Development:** CTOs are responsible for developing strategic plans that align cybersecurity with the overall business objectives of the organization.

- **Policy Formulation:** They also play a crucial role in formulating policies that enforce cybersecurity measures across all departments.

C. Collaboration with Other Executives

• **Interdepartmental Collaboration:** CTOs must work closely with other executives, such as Chief Information Security Officers (CISOs), Chief Information Officers (CIOs), and Chief Executive Officers (CEOs), to ensure a cohesive approach to cybersecurity.

• **Role in Governance:** They help govern the implementation of cybersecurity strategies, ensuring they comply with regulatory requirements and meet industry standards.

2. Best Practices for Building Cross-Functional Cybersecurity Teams

Creating an effective cybersecurity team requires strategic planning and management. This section outlines the best practices for assembling and leading a team that can robustly defend against cyber threats.

A. Team Composition

• **Diverse Expertise:** Build a team with a diverse range of skills including IT security, risk management, compliance, network engineering, and incident response.

• **Roles and Responsibilities:** Clearly define roles and responsibilities to ensure each team member knows their tasks and how they contribute to the cybersecurity goals of the organization.

B. Recruitment and Training

• **Hiring Practices:** Focus on recruiting individuals with strong technical skills and a solid understanding of cybersecurity practices. Consider candidates with varied backgrounds to bring different perspectives to the team.

• **Ongoing Training:** Provide continuous training and professional development opportunities to keep the team updated on the latest cybersecurity technologies, threats, and trends.

C. Fostering Team Collaboration

Encouraging Communication: Promote open communication within the team to ensure information flows freely and everyone can contribute to decision-making processes.

Cross-Departmental Engagements: Facilitate regular meetings with other departments to discuss cybersecurity issues and integrate security practices across the organization.

D. Implementing Effective Leadership Strategies

• **Leadership Style:** Adopt a leadership style that encourages teamwork, innovation, and accountability.

• **Performance Monitoring:** Implement key performance indicators (KPIs) to measure the effectiveness of the team and adjust strategies as necessary.

Conclusion

The importance of strategic cybersecurity leadership cannot be overstated. CTOs play a crucial role in protecting an organization from cyber threats by leading strategic initiatives and building competent, cross-functional teams. By following best practices in leadership and team management, CTOs can ensure their organizations are well-prepared to face the cybersecurity challenges of today and tomorrow. This chapter provides the foundation for developing these essential leadership qualities and team dynamics, fostering a strong cybersecurity culture within the organization.

STRATEGIC CYBERSECURITY LEADERSHIP AND CISO

In the rapidly evolving realm of cybersecurity, the role of the Chief Information Security Officer (CISO) is crucial. CISOs are responsible for overseeing the security posture of their organizations, strategizing to protect against threats, and leading teams that implement these strategies. This chapter explores the strategic leadership role of the CISO in cybersecurity initiatives and provides insights into the best practices for building and leading effective cross-functional cybersecurity teams.

1. The Strategic Role of the CISO

This section will delve into the responsibilities of a CISO and how they align with organizational goals in cybersecurity.

A. Core Responsibilities

- **Overview:** A CISO is primarily responsible for establishing and maintaining the enterprise vision, strategy, and program to ensure information assets are adequately protected.

- **Risk Management:** The CISO assesses and mitigates risks related to IT and information assets, often overseeing a risk management framework that includes identifying, evaluating, and reporting on information security risks.

B. Strategic Planning and Implementation

- **Security Strategy Development:** CISOs develop strategic plans that integrate cybersecurity with business operations, ensuring that security measures do not impede organizational goals.

- **Policy Development:** They are also key in developing and enforcing policies that comply with regulatory requirements and protect the organization from potential threats.

C. Executive Collaboration

- **Interdepartmental Leadership:** CISOs work closely with other C-suite executives to align security strategies with business objectives.

- **Board Interaction:** Regularly report to the board of directors on security strategies, threats, and initiatives to ensure top-level buy-in and support for security programs.

2. Best Practices for Building and Leading Cybersecurity Teams

Effective cybersecurity requires a skilled, motivated, and well-organized team. This section outlines how CISOs can build and lead such teams.

A. Team Composition

- **Skills Diversity:** Assemble a team with diverse skills ranging from technical expertise in threat analysis to legal knowledge for compliance and ethical guidelines.

- **Clear Roles and Responsibilities:** Define clear roles and responsibilities that align with the team's goals and individual skills.

B. Recruitment and Development

- **Talent Acquisition:** Employ rigorous recruitment processes to select individuals with not only the right skills but also a strong ethical foundation and the ability to think strategically.

- **Continuous Education:** Encourage ongoing education and certifications in cybersecurity trends and technologies to keep the team's knowledge up-to-date.

C. Promoting Team Dynamics

- **Encourage Collaboration:** Foster an environment where team members feel comfortable sharing information and ideas, ensuring collaborative problem-solving.

- **Conflict Resolution:** Develop effective strategies for resolving conflicts within the team, maintaining a focus on the organization's broader security objectives.

D. Leadership Approaches

- **Inclusive Leadership:** Adopt a leadership style that respects diverse opinions and promotes inclusiveness.

- **Performance Metrics:** Utilize key performance indicators (KPIs) to measure team effectiveness and individual contributions toward achieving cybersecurity goals.

3. Case Studies of Effective CISO Leadership

This section will provide real-world examples of CISOs who have successfully navigated the challenges of strategic cybersecurity leadership.

Case Study 1: A CISO at a multinational corporation that successfully integrated advanced threat detection technologies into the company's existing systems.

Case Study 2: A CISO in the healthcare sector who led the response to a significant data breach, minimizing damage and swiftly restoring secure operations.

4. Maintaining Leadership in a Changing Landscape

Discuss how CISOs can stay effective leaders despite the constantly evolving nature of cyber threats.

Stay Informed: Continually update oneself with the latest cybersecurity trends, threats, and defence mechanisms.

Adaptability: Be willing to adapt strategies in response to new information and changing circumstances in the cybersecurity landscape.

Conclusion

Conclude by reinforcing the importance of the CISO's role in strategic cybersecurity leadership. Highlight how effective leadership and team management are crucial for developing a resilient cybersecurity posture. Emphasize that the ongoing success of a cybersecurity program relies on the CISO's ability to lead, innovate, and adapt to new challenges. This chapter provides essential strategies and insights that help CISOs and future cybersecurity leaders navigate their roles effectively, ensuring their organizations are well-protected against potential cyber threats.

THE FUTURE OF CYBERSECURITY

As we move further into the digital age, the landscape of cybersecurity continues to evolve at an unprecedented rate. With new technologies come new vulnerabilities, making it imperative for organizations to stay ahead of threats. This chapter explores predictions for the future of cybersecurity and guides the proactive role a Chief Technology Officer (CTO) can play in shaping effective cybersecurity initiatives and policies.

1. Predictions for the Future Landscape of Cybersecurity

This section delves into emerging trends and technologies that are expected to shape the future of cybersecurity.

A. Advancements in AI and Machine Learning

• **Overview:** Discuss how AI and machine learning will continue to advance, becoming more sophisticated in predicting and mitigating cyber threats.

• **Impact:** Explain the dual-use nature of AI in cybersecurity—both as a tool for cyber defence and a potential vector for attacks.

B. Increasing Threats from IoT Devices

• **Description:** With the exponential growth of IoT devices, predict an increase in attacks targeting these devices due to their often insecure nature and the valuable data they collect.

• **Examples:** Highlight potential scenarios such as widespread DDoS attacks orchestrated through compromised IoT devices.

C. Rise of Quantum Computing

• **Explanation:** Outline how the advent of quantum computing could undermine current encryption methods, leading to a need for quantum-resistant cryptography.

• **Implications:** Discuss the race between developing quantum computing technologies and the cybersecurity measures needed to protect against them.

D. Regulatory Changes

- **Trends:** Anticipate more stringent regulations globally as data breaches and their impacts on privacy and security continue to be a significant concern.

- **Impact on Businesses:** Consider how increased regulation will affect how businesses approach data security and compliance.

2. Guidance on the Proactive Role of a CTO in Cybersecurity

This section provides actionable advice on how CTOs can take a proactive role in steering their organizations towards robust cybersecurity practices.

A. Leadership and Advocacy

- **Strategic Leadership:** Emphasize the CTO's role in advocating for and leading the charge on implementing advanced cybersecurity technologies and strategies.

- **Policy Advocacy:** Discuss the importance of the CTO's involvement in shaping policies that not only comply with regulations but also anticipate future cybersecurity challenges.

B. Fostering Innovation

- **Encouraging R&D:** Guide CTOs on setting up dedicated research and development teams to innovate security solutions that address both current and future threats.

- **Collaboration:** Stress the importance of collaborating with industry peers, academic institutions, and cybersecurity think tanks to stay ahead of security trends.

C. Building a Future-Ready Cybersecurity Team

- **Skills Development:** Provide strategies for developing a team with the skills to handle next-generation cybersecurity challenges, including training in AI, machine learning, and quantum computing.

- **Recruitment and Retention:** Offer best practices for attracting and retaining top cybersecurity talent in a competitive market.

D. Proactive Risk Management

- **Continuous Assessment:** Outline methods for continuous risk assessment and the integration of adaptive security architectures that can respond dynamically to threats.

- **Investment in Technology:** Advice on strategic investments in technology that will provide long-term security benefits, such as advanced threat detection systems and secure cloud services.

Conclusion

Conclude the chapter by reinforcing the critical role of CTOs in navigating the future cybersecurity landscape. Highlight the necessity of proactive strategies and continuous innovation in cybersecurity practices to protect against emerging threats. Summarize the key points discussed and encourage CTOs to take a forward-thinking approach to cybersecurity, ensuring their organizations remain resilient in the face of future challenges.

FUTURE CHALLENGES IN CYBERSECURITY

Increasingly Sophisticated Cyberattacks:

Cyber threats are becoming more sophisticated and harder to detect. Hackers are using artificial intelligence (AI) and machine learning (ML) to carry out attacks that can learn and adapt, making them more effective against traditional security measures.

Expanding Attack Surfaces:

With the growth of IoT devices and the broader adoption of cloud computing, the attack surface for cyber threats is rapidly expanding. More connected devices mean more potential entry points for attackers.

Privacy and Data Protection:

As data continues to be a crucial asset, protecting it from breaches will be more challenging. Regulations like GDPR have started to shape data protection practices, but the increasing volume and sensitivity of data collected will continue to test these boundaries.

Emerging Technologies and Their Implications

Quantum Computing:

Experts believe quantum computing could break many of the encryption methods that currently protect our data. Organizations should start preparing by researching quantum-resistant cryptography to safeguard information against future quantum-enabled threats.

AI and Machine Learning in Defense:

Just as AI and ML can be used for attacks, they are also powerful tools for cybersecurity defence. Automated systems that can detect and respond to threats in real time will become a staple in cybersecurity strategies.

Blockchain for Security:

Blockchain technology is being explored for its potential to enhance security, particularly in terms of data integrity and transparency. Its application could revolutionize how we manage identity verification and secure transactions.

Expert Opinions and Preparing for the Future

Stay Informed and Train Continuously:

Cybersecurity is a field that continuously evolves. Staying informed about the latest trends, threats, and technologies is crucial. Regular training and updating of skills for IT professionals and general staff can help an organization stay one step ahead of potential cyber threats.

Implement Robust Security Frameworks:

Experts suggest adopting robust security frameworks that can evolve with your organization and its technological landscape. This involves not only investing in technology but also in creating policies that address the human element of cybersecurity.

Focus on Resilience and Recovery:

As it becomes harder to prevent all attacks, focusing on resilience—how quickly and effectively you can respond and recover from an attack—will be critical. Developing comprehensive incident response plans and conducting regular drills to test these plans is essential.

Expert Insight:

Cybersecurity experts stress the importance of integrating security practices into the development phase of any product or system, rather than treating security as an afterthought. This approach, known as "security by design," ensures that security measures are built into the infrastructure of IT projects from the ground up.

Conclusion

Preparing and proactive adaptation are key as we navigate future challenges and opportunities in cybersecurity. By understanding the potential changes and implementing forward-thinking security measures, individuals and organisations can protect themselves against emerging threats and leverage new technologies to enhance their security posture. This strategic approach to cybersecurity will be fundamental to thriving in an increasingly connected and digital world.

www.ingramcontent.com/pod-product-compliance
Lightning Source LLC
LaVergne TN
LVHW051641050326
832903LV00022B/847